Another outtake of the famous battle that was fought above our cities and in our skies.

BATTLE OF BRITAIN

PAUL CORFIELD

BATTLE OF BRITAIN

another out take of the famous battle that was fought above our cities and our skies

July 10th 1940 — October 31 1940

PAUL CORFIELD

Copyright @2021 by PAUL CORFIELD

All rights reserved. No part of this book may be reproduced in any form or by any electronic or mechanical means, including information storage and retrieval systems, without permission in writing from the publisher, except by reviewers, who may quote brief passages in a review.

This publication contains the opinions and ideas of its author. It is intended to provide helpful and informative material on the subjects addressed in the publication. The author and publisher specifically disclaim all responsibility for any liability, loss or risk, personal or otherwise, which is incurred as a consequence, directly or indirectly, of the use and application of any of the contents of this book.

WORKBOOK PRESS LLC
187 E Warm Springs Rd,
Suite B285, Las Vegas, NV 89119, USA

Website:	https://workbookpress.com/
Hotline:	1-888-818-4856
Email:	admin@workbookpress.com

Ordering Information:
Quantity sales. Special discounts are available on quantity purchases by corporations, associations, and others. For details, contact the publisher at the address above.

ISBN-13: 978-1-955459-84-6 (Paperback Version)
          978-1-955459-85-3 (Digital Version)

REV. DATE: 11.06.2021

CONTENTS

INTRODUCTION 007

1 008

2 016

3 021

4 033

5 060

6 066

7 113

RECAP OF BATTLE OF BRITAIN 120

CREDITATIONS 122

BIBLIOGRAPHY 125

INDEX

1..................The start of The Battle.

2..................The hardest day.

3..................7 September.

4..................Phases of the battle.

5..................Dowding system.

6..................Groups and squadrons.

7..................11 group RAF.

8..................British Home Front.

9..................German Aircraft.

10..................Commander and leaders (British).

11..................Commander and leaders (German).

12..................Operations during the Battle.

13..................Key points of battle.

INTRODUCTION

Although The Battle of Britain was 75 years ago. It is still a massive part of British history, and the great British public all recognize that if it had not been for. "the few". Who fought in the skies over this great land, and is still a topic of interest to a lot of us and in schools around Britain. We all give thanks to those that fought and died for us during this time.

1

On June 17 1940, The French signed an armistice and pulled out of World War 2, after being defeated by Hitler's Nazi Germany which had conquered most of Western Europe in less than two months. But British Prime Minister Winston Churchill rallied his stubborn people, and out-manuovered those politicians who wanted to negotiate with Adolf Hitler. But Britain's success in continuing the war very much depended on the RAF Fighter Command's agility to thwart the Luftwaffe's efforts to gain air superiority, This then would be the first all air battle in history.

The Germans had poor intelligence and little idea of British vulnerabilities. They wasted most of July waiting for a British surrender and attacked in august. Although airstrikes did substantial damage to radar sites, on 13-15 August the Luftwaffe soon abandoned that avenue and turned to attacks on RAF bases.

The first of the German bombing raids took place on 10 July 1940, At first the Luftwaffe started by closing the English channel to Merchant shipping then he bombed ships in the English channel and coastal defences, then they concentrated on destroying the RAF. The Luftwaffe tempted the RAF out for a full scale battle. The name Battle of Britain, is taken from Winston Churchill's speech which he said "THE BATTLE OF FRANCE IS OVER, THE

BATTLE OF BRITAINF IS ABOUT TO BIGIN". The German codename for the British invasion was called "Operation Sea Lion". By the end of July the RAF had lost 150 aircraft to that of the Luftwaffe who lost 268.

For any likelihood of success the operation required both air and naval superiority over the English Channel, neither of which the Germans ever achieved during or after the Battle.

In August the Luftwaffe started to attack Fighter Commands airfields, operation rooms and radar stations the idea was to destroy the RAF on the ground so that the Luftwaffe need not fight them in the air. Without radar the RAF would be seriously hampered in terms of early warning, Destruction of the operation rooms would cut off all communications between fighter bases and those at the heart of controlling the movement of fighter planes, destroying runways would hamper chances of take-offs.

August 15 1940 was is seen as key date, bad weather stopped the Luftwaffe which had launched its biggest operation to date, with RAF airfields a primary target. Nearly all the Stuka dive bombers were destroyed by this date as they fell easy prey for the British fighter planes, making it all but impossible for pin-point bombing of radar stations.

The major attack was launched by two waves, totalling approximately 100 enemy aircraft, against the fighter station of Hawkinge in Kent. Pilot Officer J A A Gibson led a section of no: 501 squadron Hurricanes from Hawkinge to intercept the attack. Gibson sighted one formation of about twenty Junkers J U 87 dive bombers approaching from the south, and attacking from out of the sun he sent it into the sea in flames, then he noticed other dive-bombers attacking his home airfield. He returned at speed in time to intercept two and damage one of them. Their rear gunners, however, set his Hurricane on fire, but noticing that he was near the town of Folkestone., Gibson stayed with his burning aircraft and steered it clear of the town before finally jumping at a height of 1000 feet. He was awarded an immediate D.F.C (Distinguished Flying Cross), for his courage.

Essential British airfields were pitted with bomb craters, the RAF's effectiveness was further decreased by bomb damage to its radar stations and operation centres which were unfortunately sited on airfields, Aircraft were being destroyed on the ground, and it was becoming difficult to co-ordinate formations in the air. Losses of aircraft were turning into Germans favour.

On August 18 1940 was known as The Hardest Day of the battle of Britain because both sides suffered their heaviest losses. The Luftwaffe made an all-out effort to severely damage Fighter Command. The air battle On August 18 1940 was known as The Hardest Day of the battle of Britain because both sides suffered their heaviest losses, The Luftwaffe made an all-out effort to severely damage Fighter Command. The air battle that took place on this date were among the largest aerial engagements in history at that time.

The British outperformed the Luftwaffe in the air,

Achieving a favourable ratio or 2-1, However, around six to eight fighters and other RAF aircraft were caught and destroyed on the ground, both sides lost more aircraft combined on this day than at any other point during the campaign, including Battle of Britain day.

One of the aircraft lost on this day was a 501 Squadron hurricane flown by Squadron leader Kenneth Hawkeye Lee who hit by German ace Gerhard Shortfall. With his plane engulfed in flames and falling from the skies and badly injured, he managed to turn his plane on its back and fall to safety, landing in a cornfield, his plane crashed into a field in Whitstable Kent at 350 mph. there were 136 RAF planes destroyed or damaged, 4 of them from 501 squadron (Hurricanes) based at Gravesend crashed near Whitstable around lunchtime.

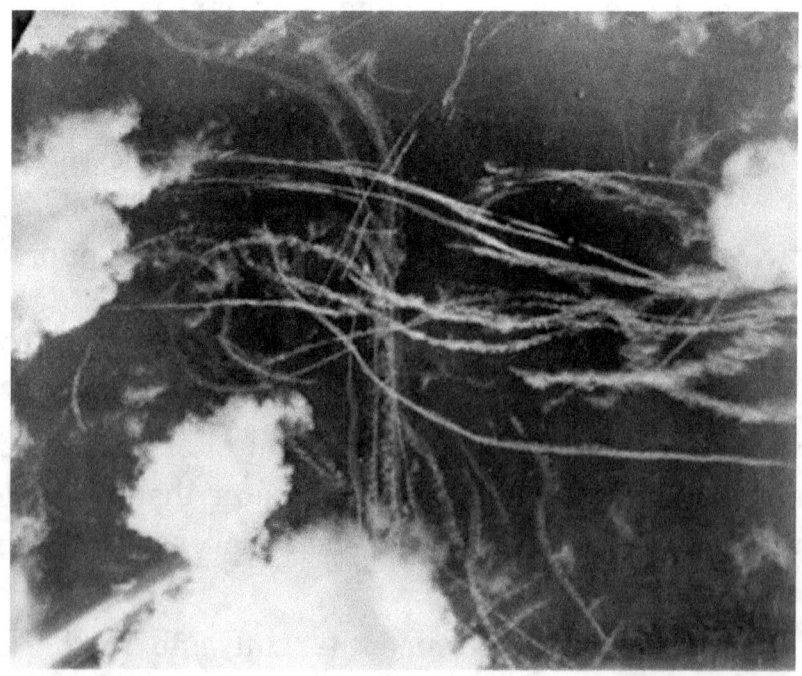

British and German aircraft trails after a dog-fight

German intelligence suggested that the RAF had only 300 serviceable fighters, taking into consideration German pilots claims and there estimates of British production capabilities. Where as in fact there were 855 machines serviceable with 289 at storage units with another 84 at training units, giving a total of 1,438 fighters, twice as many than at beginning of July 1940.

Expecting weakening opposition, the Luftwaffe prepared for a major action against the RAF sector stations, there plan of attack was simple, German bombers were to strike the RAF airfields in the south east corner of England. The most important airfields in this region, Tangmere was in the South-East near the coast at Chichester, Debden was in the North near Saffron Walden. Each of these airfields housed two to three squadrons and had its own sector operations room.

From there its fighters were directed from its satellite into combat. There were six satellite airfields at, Westhampnett, Croydon, Gravesend, Manson, Rochford and RAF Martlesham Heath, Manston and martlesham Heath each housed two squadrons, the remainder each housed one. There was also RAF Hawkinge, just inland from Folkestone. Not all of these airfields were targeted on 18 august.

The following targets were chosen for attack 18 August 1940...

German Bomber Units	Target
I .Kampfgeschwaider 1 (kg1)	RAF Biggin Hill
III .Kampfgeschwaider 53 (kg53)	RAF Kenley and RAF North Weald
I and II.kampfgeschwaider 54 (kg54)	Fleet Air Arm Base RAF Gosport
I, II,and III kampfgeschwaider 76	RAF Kenley and RAF Biggin Hill
I,II, and II Sturzkampfgeschwaider 77	Poling radar station RAF Ford Thornley island
Kampfgeschwaider 2 (kg2)	RAF Hornchurch
II.Kampfgeschwaider 27 (kg27)	Liverpool Docks 1
Sturzcampfgeschwaider 3	RAF Gosport

In August Operation Adeirangriff (Eagle Attack) was launched against RAF airfields in southern England. By the first week in September, the Luftwaffe had not gained the results desired by Hitler, Frustrated by this the Germans turned towards the strategic bombings of cities, an offensive which was aimed at British military and civil industries, but all so civilian morale. The attacks began on September 7 1940 but were to reach there daylight climax on 15 September on this day the Luftwaffe launched its largest most concentrated attack against London in the hope of drawing out the RAF into a battle of annihilation.

Around 1'500 aircraft took part in the air battles which lasted till dusk, this action was the climax of the battle of Britain. While the Luftwaffe had suffered unexpectedly high loss ratio prior to 15 September, they had learned one key thing. If they flew at a high altitude they had on occasions taken fighter command by surprise, that was all they knew, German intelligence had failed to discover that the radar stations that were dotted around southern and eastern England were only effective up to 20,000 feet, Luftwaffe pilots simply believed it was because fighter commands spitfires and hurricanes took time to reach high altitudes, however, to a degree this was immaterial.

What they had learned was the higher they flew the better chance of success they would have. Staff officers of Luftwaffe 2 based in Brussels began planning a two-pronged offensive on 15 September the targets were purely military. The first target selected was the Battersea railway station (w l e r) West London Extension Railway, in Battersea district. The tracks were 12 abreast in some places and linked to London to take heavy industries of the West Midlands and other industrial cities in the north and south east of Britain.

2

The German high command had planned to issue new orders for operation sea lion on September 17. Therefore control of the skies were vital if the plan was to proceed and invading barges to be safe from attacks from the RAF. On 14 September the commander of the Luftwaffe, Hermann Goering had sent instructions that an all-out aerial assault was to be made on southern England on September 15.

The second target for the Luftwaffe, for the larger attack during the afternoon, the dock areas of the Thames Estuary including the warehouse of the East end of London, Surrey Commercial Docks, south of the river, and Royal Docks, (royal Victoria dock, west India docks, Royal albert dock and king George v dock).

On 7 September 1940 THE BLITZ, Nazi bomber planes launched an attack on London, killing an estimated 450 people in day and night raids, More than 100 tons of high explosives were dropped on 16 British cities over a period of 276days (almost 37 weeks). London was attacked 71 times, Birmingham, Liverpool and Plymouth 8 times. Bristol 6 times. Glasgow 5 times. Southampton 4times. Portsmouth and hull 3 times. There was at least one raid on another eight cities. This was a result of a rapid escalation starting on 24 august 1940.

Starting 7 September London was bombed by the Luftwaffe for 57 consecutive nights, More than 1 million London houses were destroyed or damaged and more than 40'000 civilians were killed, almost half of them in

London. In September alone the Luftwaffe dropped 5'300 tonnes of high explosives on the capital in just 24 nights, in the efforts to "soften up" the British population and to destroy morale before the planned invasion, German planes extended their targets to include the major coastal ports and centres of production and supply outside London were heavily bombed, the major Atlantic sea port of Liverpool was also heavily bombed, causing nearly 4'000 deaths within the Merseyside area during the war. The North Sea port of Hull a convenient and easily found primary and secondary target for bombers unable to locate their primary targets was subject to 86 raids.

It was a little past 8pm. British military units were alerted with the codename Cromwell, meaning that the German invasion had begun. A state of emergency broke out in England: even home defence unit were put to the ready. During the night of 7/8 September attacks extended over many hours covered a considerable area of London and were of an intense nature. Over 600 Fire appliances were in operation during the night. Other ports including, Belfast, Cardiff, Portsmouth, Plymouth, Southampton, and Sheffield. Birmingham and Coventry were heavily targeted because of the Spitfire and Tank factories in Coventry, the centre of Coventry was almost completely destroyed.

A massive series of raids involving nearly four hundred bombers and more than six hundred fighters targeted docks in the east end of London day and night. The raids were codenamed operation lodge. The RAF anticipated attacks on airfields and 11 group rose to meet them, in greater numbers than the Luftwaffe expected. The first official deployment of 12groups Lee-Mallory's Big Wing took twenty minute to form up, missing its intended target, but encountered another formation of bombers while still climbing.

Fighter pilot Ray Holmes was out of ammunition after downing another plane when he spotted a German bomber heading for Buckingham palace so he decided to fly his Hurricane directly into the German Dornier bomber and disabled it, the bomber went down into Victoria station while his aircraft crashed into a nearby street Holmes bailed out shortly after the impact. He took the Dornier's tail off with his wing on it went down nose first, then he realised that it had damaged his aerodynamics and bailed out his plane crashed on Buckingham palace road. And he came to rest dangling from a 3 story house.

The most damaging aspect to the Luftwaffe targeting London was the increase in range, the bf109e escorts had limited fuel capacity resulting in only a 660km (410mile) maximum range solely on internal fuel, when they arrived having only 10 minutes of flying time left before turning for home, leaving the bomber un defended by fighter escorts. The Luftwaffe began to abandon their morning raids with attacks on London Starting late in the afternoon. A Junkers JU88 returning from a raid on London was shot down in Kent on 27 September resulting in the Battle of Graveney marsh the last action between British and Foreign military forces on British mainland soil.

The Battle can roughly be divided into four phases...

3

The Kanalkapf comprised a series of fights over convoys in the English Channel. It was launched partly because Kesselring and Sperrie were not sure about what to do, the RAF and Luftwaffe skirmished over the channel, and these engagements saw German Stuka's attacking British coastal convoys rather than waste pilots and planes defending them.

He was blocked by Churchill and the Royal Navy who refused to symbolically cease control of the channel as the fight continued, the Germans introduced there twin engine bombers which were escorted by Messerschmitt fighters. These battles off the coast tended to favour the Germans, whose bomber escorts had the advantage of altitude and outnumbered the RAF fighters. From9 July reconnaissance probing by Denier do17 bomber put severe strain on the RAF pilots and machines, with high losses to BF109's, when nine 141 Squadron defiants went into action on 19 July six were lost to 109's before a squadron of hurricanes intervened.

Due to the proximity of the German airfield to the coast, the fighter of 11 group of ten did not have sufficient warning in order to block these attacks. On 25 July a coal convoy and escorting destroyers suffered such heavy losses to attacks by Stuka dive bombers that the Admiralty decided convoys should travel at night: The RAF shot down 16 raiders but lost 7 aircraft. By 8 August 1940 18 coal ships and 4 destroyers had been sunk, but the navy was determined to send a convoy of 20 ships through rather than move coal by railway. After repeated Stuka attacks that day six ships were badly damaged, four were sunk and only 4 reached their destination. The RAF lost 14 fighters and shot down 31 German aircraft.

The navy now cancelled all further convoys through the channel and sent coal by rail, even so these early combat encounters provided both sides with experience. The Luftwaffe was supported by e-boats of the kriegsmarine (German navy), During June and July fighter command lost 96 fighters while downing 227 German aircraft.

The result of this battle was limited German Victory.

Phase 2 12-23 August Adlerangriff (Eagle Attack).

The early assault against coastal airfields. The essential target was RAF fighter command, the services destruction would deny the British their air superiority asset. Throughout July and early August the made preparations for adlertag the date of the assault was postponed several times because of bad weather, it was carried out on 13 August 1940.

On 12 August the first attempt was made to blind the dowding system, when aircraft from the specialised fight bomber unit Erprobungruppe 210 attacked four radar stations, three were briefly taken off the air but were back working within six hours. The raids appeared to show that British radars were difficult to knock out.

The failure to mount follow up attacks allowed the RAF to get the stations back on the air, and the Luftwaffe neglected strikes on the supporting infrastructures, such as phone lines and power stations, which could have rendered the radars useless. Even if the towers themselves (which were very difficult to destroy) remained intact.

Adlertag (Eagle day) opened with a series of attacks led by epro 210 on costal airfields used as forward landing grounds for the RAF fighters, as well as satellite airfields (including Manston and Hawkinge). As the week drew on the airfield attacks moved further inland, and repeated raids were made on radar chains.

The German attacks on 13 August inflicted significant damage and casualties on the ground, but marred with poor intelligence and communication, they did not make a significant impression on fighter command, but Adlertag and the following operations failed to destroy the RAF. The small number of British fighters that goring had encountered in July and early August convinced him that fighter command was operating with around 300-400 aircraft. British fighters downed 31 German aircraft for a loss of 21 of their own.

Believing that they had caused significant damage on 12 August, the Germans began their offensive the next day. The skies were grey and the atmosphere was misty, so goring attempted to postpone the operation unfortunately for the Luftwaffe, not all squadrons received the message. One of the attack groups carried on with only bombers, as the bomber crews had no idea that they had no escorts until they were intercepted by fighters from 74 squadron RAF who shot down 5 bombers and seriously damaged a further five. A raid by a group of JU87 Stuka dive bombers also suffered heavy casualties due to breakdown in communication.

German bomber unit TargetKampfgeschwader 1 (KG 1)RAF Biggin Hill Kampfgeschwader 76(KG 76) RAF Kenley RAF Debden /RAF Biggin Hill / Other unknown targets Kampfgeschwader 2 (KG 2)RAF Hornchurch / RAF Eastchurch /Manston Kampfgeschwader (KG 3) RAF Eastchurch Kampfgeschwader 53(KG 53)RAF North Weald Erprobungsgruppe 210Radar Stations; Rye, Pevensey, Dover. RAF Hawkinge/RAF Manston/ RAF Kenley Kampfgeschwader 4 (KG 4) Unknown targets (lack of records)/some mine laying operations in English Channel. Kampfgeschwader 40(KG 40)Dishforth Kampfgeschwader(KG 26)RAF Dishforth /Linton-on-Ouse Kampfgeschwader 30(KG 30)RAF Driffield Kampfgeschwader 27(KG 27)Ports of Bristol/Birkenhead/Liverpool Lehrgeschwader 1 (LG 1) RAF Worthy Down / Ports of Southampton, Portsmouth and surrounding airfields RAF Detling/Other unspecified operations Sturzkampfgeschwader 3(StG 3)StG 3 was to take part. For unknown reasons it was removed from the order of battle on 13 August. Another source asserts that the unit had its missions cancelled owing to poor weather. Kampfgeschwader 51(KG 51)RAF Bibury/Spithead harbour/Ventnor radar stationKampfgeschwader 54(KG 54)Fleet Air Arm base Gosport[59]/RAF Croydon[RAF Farnborough RAF Odiham Kampfgeschwader 55(KG 55)Plymouth/Feltham[64]/RAF Middle Wallop Sturzkampfgeschwader 1(StG 1)RAF Warmwell[14]/RAF

Detling I., and II./Sturzkampfgeschwader 2 (StG 2)Portland area and airfields/RAF Middle Wallop/RAF Warmwell/YeovilSturzkampfgeschwader 77 (StG 77)RAF Warmwell/Portland.

In the afternoon as weather cleared Goring gave the word to launch the major attack. They struck a variety of targets across southern Britain but inflicted little lasting damage, Raids continued on and off the next day, opposed in squadron strength by fighter command. On 19 August 1940 Goring ordered attacks on aircraft.

On aircraft factories. On 23 August he ordered that RAF airfields be attacked. That evening an attack was mounted on a tyre factory in Birmingham. Raids continued through 24 August.

Phase 3

24 August—6 September 1940. The Luftwaffe targets the airfields. The critical phase of the battle. Portsmouth was hit by a major attack, that night several areas of London were bombed: the east end was set ablaze and bombs landed on central London. The RAF bombed Berlin on the night of 25-26 August, sending 95 aircraft to bomb Tempelhof airport near the centre of Berlin and Siemensstadt. Of which 81 dropped their bombs in and around Berlin, these bombings hurt Goring's pride, as he had previously stated that the British would never be able to bomb the city.

Bomb Damage in Central London during the Battle of Britain 1940

From 24 August onwards, the battle was a fight between Kesselring's Luftwaffe 2 and parks 11 group, the Luftwaffe concentrated all their strengths on knocking out fighter command and made repeated attacks on airfields. Of the 33 heavy attacks in the following two weeks, 24 were against airfields. The key sector stations were hit repeatedly:

Biggin Hill and Hornchurch four times each: Debden and North Weald twice each Croydon, Gravesend, Rochford, Hawkinge and Manston were also attacked in strength. Coastal commands east church was bombed at least seven times because it was believed to be a fighter command aerodrome. Biggin Hill was worst hit on 31 August and the vital control room was knocked out of action. The fighter command also suffered its heaviest losses of the battle that day, with 38 aircraft shot down, the benefits of the RAF's home advantage can be seen very clearly that day. Of the 38 pilots shot down 9 pilots were killed, most of them wounded and put out of action, but were able to return to the battle almost immediately. In contrast very few of the 39 German aircraft crew lost on the same day will have escaped to fight again.

To offset some losses, some 58 Fleet air arm pilot volunteers were seconded to RAF squadrons, and a similar number of Fairey battle pilots were used. Most replacements from Operation Training units (o t u's) had as little as nine hours flying time and no gunnery or air-to-air combat training. At this point, the Multinational nature of fighter command came to the forehand, many squadrons and personnel from the air forces of the Dominions were already attached to the RAF, including top level commanders. Australians, Canadians, New Zealanders, Rhodesians, and South Africans. In addition, there were other nationalities represented, including Free French, Belgian and a Jewish pilot from the British mandate of Palestine.

They were bolstered by the arrival of fresh Czechoslovak and Polish squadrons. 303 Polish squadron was from 2 August 1940 based at RAF Northolt and became operational on 31 August, at the onset, serving RAF officers were appointed to serve as C.O, S/L, R G Kellett and fighter commanders, F/L, J A Kent and F/L A S Forbes alongside the poles, as they were unfamiliar with RAF fighter commands language, procedures and training. The squadron was equipped Hawker Hurricane fighter aircraft, after a period of training on 24 August 1940, the squadron was scrambled for the first time, although it did not come into contact with enemy aircraft.

30 August 1940 saw 303 squadron score its first victory while still officially being non-operational, when during a training flight F/O Ludwick Paskewicz shot down a German Messerschmitt BF110 of 4. Zg76 and they were declared operational the next day. 303 squadron became the highest scoring allied unit.

Phase 4

7 September onwards, the day attacks switch to British

towns and cities.

Bombing raid statistics. As follows.

City	Tonnage of high explosive dropped	No: of major raids
London	18,291	71
Liverpool/Merseyside	1,957	8
Birmingham	1,852	8
Glasgow/Clydeside	1,329	5
Plymouth	1,228	8
Bristol	919	6
Coventry	818	2
Portsmouth	687	3
Southampton	647	4
Hull	593	3
Manchester	578	3
Belfast	440	2
Sheffield	355	1
Newcastle	155	1
Nottingham	137	1
Cardiff	115	1

This is a table showing by city and number of raids, (where at least 100 tons of bombs were dropped).

The first deliberate air raids on London were mainly aimed to The Port of London, causing severe damage. On 17 September the British had their first hints that the immediate threat of invasion was gone, if we look at the total fighter production between 17 August and 14 September we will see that 43 Defiants, 271 Hurricanes, 186 Spitfires, 26 buffalo's and 3 western whirlwinds were produced giving fighter command a total of 1154 serviceable aircraft, this is an average daily total output of 3606 meaning that Beaverbrook's factories were producing a little over twice as many fighter aircraft that were being shot down.

In the second half of September German tactics changed once again, there were still two major daylight raids on 27 and 30 September, but neither were successful, the attack on 30 September was the last large scale daylight raid on London. The night-time raids continued, while during the day the Germans began to carry out a large number of fighter-bomber raids.

From 1– 31 October the Germans abandon large scale daylight raids, instead they focus on small scale low level by JU88's and high-level fighter bomber raids, using bomb-carrying BF109's supported by pure fighters, the BF110 was also used as a fighter-bomber during this phase of the battle.

1 October 1940 Germans sent small raids of 20-70 aircraft to attack airfields in England, London was not bombed during the day. The Germans lost 4 fighters while the British lost 5 fighters and pilots were killed, London was bombed at night at 06.30 a JU88 bomber landed at Brightlingsea, Essex when the pilot became lost in the darkness during an early morning reconnaissance mission

and was captured.

During the day the Luftwaffe launched 6 raids of BF109and BF110 fighters and fighter-bombers against London and Kent, the Germans lost 5 bombers and 5 fighters, while the British lost just 1 aircraft without the loss of the pilot.

4

The Dowding system was the first integrated air defence battle management system in the world, controlling the airspace across the UK from Northern Scotland to the South Coast. Report from CH radars and the Observer corps were sent directly to fighter command headquarters (F C H Q) at Bentley priory where they were 'filtered' to combine multiple reports of the same formations in single tracks, Telephone operators would then forward only the information of interest to the group headquarters, where the map would be re-created. The system was built by the Royal Air Force just before the start of WW2 and proved decisive in the Battle of Britain. The re-created map could then be relayed to commanders so they could see how best to deploy there forces quickly and without clutter, instructions were relayed to pilots only from the squadrons sector control rooms, (normally co-located at the fighters operating bases.) to intercept as well as to return them to base. Sector stations also controlled the Anti-Aircraft Batteries in the area.

The Dowding system is considered key to the success of the RAF against the German Air Force (Luftwaffe) during the battle of Britain, because it dramatically improved the speed and accuracy of information to the pilots. During the early part of it was expected that an average interception mission might have a 30% chance of ever seeing their target, during the battle the Dowding system maintained and average rate of over 75% with several examples of 100% rates meaning every fighter dispatched found and intercepted its target.

Organised action plan

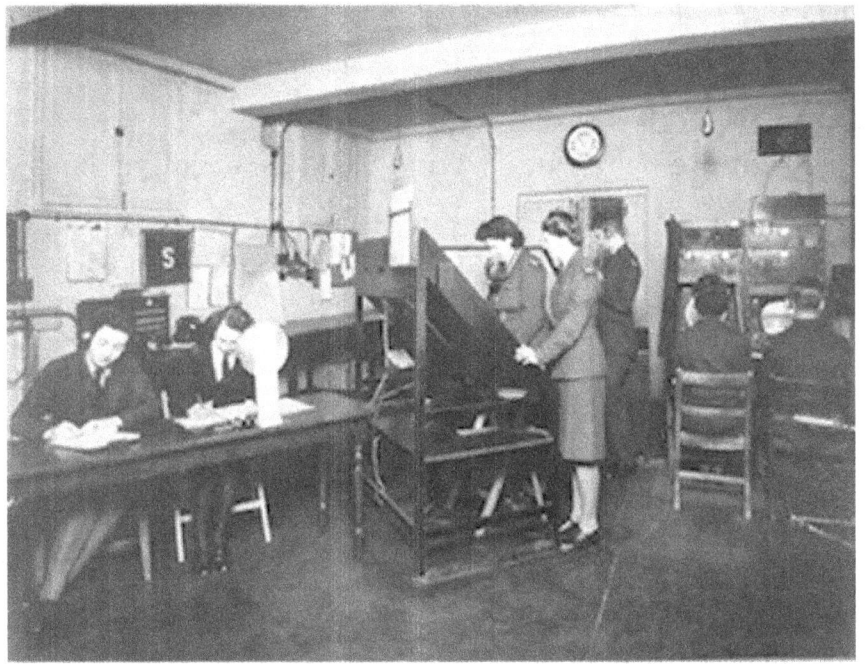

Receiver room 525

Locking their own direction system, Luftwaffe fighters had little information on the location of their RAF counterparts. And often returned to the base having never seen them, when they did, the RAF fighters were almost always in an advantageous position. Although many histories of the Battle of Britain comment on the role of the radar, it was only in conjunction with the Dowding system that radar could be truly effective.

This saw not lost on Winston Churchill who noted that.....

All the ascendancy of the Hurricanes and Spitfires would have been fruitless but for this system which has been devised and built before the war. It had shaped and refined inconstant action, and all now fused together into a most elaborate instrument of war, the like of which exists nowhere in the world.

Quantitive methods: scheduling, signal detection and target prediction.

Maximise fighter utilization through scheduling: launch fighters so as to maximize time in the air, allowing one British aircraft to fight off multiple waves of enemy aircraft with limited fuel supply.

Target prediction: With 500mph closing speeds for aircraft, enemy course prediction needed to be real time and very accurate.

Trigonometry: Dowding created a network of 1'400 trained spotters who used trigonometry to calculate the altitude of enemy aircraft.

Signal detection: Identified aircraft on radar readouts distinguished friends from foe and determining number of aircraft.

Data visualization: All radar data, spotter observations, aircraft movements and engagements were plotted in real time.

Quantification of benefits:

"At times, the dowding system achieved interception rates exceeding 80%"

The invasion of Great Britain (operation sea lion) was postponed indefinitely.

The RAF were outnumbered 2-1, but they fought off the Luftwaffe. It could therefore be claimed that the Dowding System was a force multiplier that at minimum doubled in strength.

Fuel economy: This may be trivial, but the RAF used 100 octane fuel imported from the United States. It enhanced the performance of the aircraft but it also made fight fuel a scares resource to be optimized, so it wasn't feasible to have aircraft on constant patrol, the Dowding system was fuel optimal.

Bomber command and Coastal command aircraft flew offensive sorties against targets in Germany and France during the battle, they operated in disrupting enemy shipping, Coastal Command attacked shipping and mined waters around invasion ports. While Bomber Command changed targeting priority on 3 June 1940 to attack the German aircraft industries. On 4 July the Air Ministry gave Bomber Command orders to attack ports and shipping. By September, the build-up of invasion barges in the channel ports had become a top priority target, 7 September 1940 the government issued a warning that the invasion could be expected within the next few weeks and, that night bomber command attacked the channel ports and supply dumps.

On 13 September they carried out another large raid on the channel ports. Sinking 80 large barges in the port of Ostend. 84 barges were sunk in Dunkirk after another raid on 17 September and by 19 September, almost 200 barges had been sunk. The loss of these barges may have contributed to Hitler's decision to postpone Operation Sea-Lion indefinitely.

The Bristol Blenheim units also raided German occupied airfields throughout July to December 1940, both during the daylight hours and at night, although most of these raids were unproductive, there were some successes, 1 August, 5 out of 12 Blenheim's sent to attack Haamstede and Evere (Brussels) were able to bomb, destroying or heavily damaging three BF109's of II.jg27 and apparently killing a Staffelkapitan identified as Hauptmann Albrecht Von Ankum-Frank. Two other 109's were damaged by Blenheim gunners. There were some missions which produced an almost 100% casualty rate amongst the Blenheim's.

Coastal Command directed its attention towards the protection of British shipping, and the destruction of enemy shipping. As invasion became more likely, it participated in the strikes on French harbours and airfields, laying mines and mounting numerous reconnaissance missions over the enemy held coast, in all some 9'180 sorties were flown by bombers from July to October 1940, fighter command expected to face only bombers over Britain, a series of "fighting area tactics" were formulated and rigidly adhered to involving a series of manoeuvres designed to concentrate a squadrons fire power to bring down bombers, RAF fighters flew in tight V-shaped formations (vics) of three, with four such "sections" in tight formations. Fighter command recognised the weakness of this structure early in the battle.

The German pilots dubbed the RAF formations as idiotenreichen ("rows of idiots"), because they left squadrons vulnerable to attack. Frontline RAF pilots were acutely aware of their own tactics. A compromise was adopted whereby squadron formations used much looser formations with one or two "weavers" flying independently above and behind to provide increased observation and rear protection: these tended to be the least experienced men and often the first to be shot down without the other pilots even noticing they were under attack. 74 squadron under squadron leader Adolph "Sailor" Malan adopted a variation of the German formation called "fours in line astern" which was a vast improvement on the old three aircraft, "VIC". Mallon's formation was later generally used by fighter command.

The weight of the battle fell upon 11 group, which consisted of 27 squadrons, and 8 sector and 18 airfields, which was commanded by Air vice Marshall Keith Park.

Sector A.

RAF Tangmere (sector HQ), had four squadrons, four different aircraft (fighter) 2 squadrons based there.

RAF Westhampnett. 1 squadron based there.

Sector B.

RAF Kenley. 2 squadrons based there.

RAF Redhill. Had 30 squadrons fly from there.

Sector C.

RAF Biggin Hill (sector HQ). Had 4 squadrons, 2 types of aircraft and 3 squadron based there (1 squadron was not based there).

There was also RAF

Hawkinge that had 2 squadron based there for a short period during this battle and RAF Friston in this sector.

This aerodrome was disused during the battle of Britain.

Sector D.

RAF Biggin Hill

RAF Hornchurch.

Had 4 squadrons, (1 night fighter) 3 types of aircraft, 4 squadrons were Based there.

RAF Rochford and Manston were also in sector D

Sector E.

RAF North Weald. (Sector HQ). Had 3 squadrons, 2 types of aircraft, and only 1 squadron based there.

RAF Stapleford Tawney. Had one squadron based there.

Sector F.

North Weald

RAF Debden. (Sector HQ). Had 4 squadrons, 2 types of aircraft, only 2 squadrons based there.

RAF Wimbish was also in sector F.

Sector Y.

Middle Wallop

RAF Middle Wallop. (Sector HQ). Had 1 squadron from 11 group, had Hurricane aircraft.

RAF Odiham. Was in sector Y.

Sector Z

RAF Northolt

RAF Northolt (Sector HQ). Had 5 squadrons, 2 types of aircraft, and 4 squadrons based there,

RAF Hendon, had 1 squadron from 11 Group flying Hawker Hurricanes.

This is an abbreviated account taken from stations and squadrons list.

A closer look at the airfields of 11 group during the Battle of Britain 1940.

RAF Tangmere housed the following squadrons and aircraft during the battle.

Squadron no:	Date From:	Equipped with:
145	10 May 1940	Hawker Hurricanes
43	31 May 1940	Hawker Hurricanes
601	17 June 1940	Hawker Hurricanes
1	23 June 1940	Hawker Hurricanes
266	9 August 1940	Supermarine Spitfire
17	19 August 1940	Hawker Hurricanes

607	1 September 1940	Hawker Hurricanes
601	2 September 1940	Hawker Hurricanes
213	2 September 1940	Hawker Hurricanes
145	9 October 1940	Hawker Hurricanes

Group			Area of Operations
9 Group	RAF Barton Hall, Preston, Lancashire	Not yet appointed	Not yet defined
10 Group	RAF Box,[1] Box, Wiltshire	Air Vice-Marshal Sir C J Quintin Brand	South West England and South Wales
11 Group	RAF Uxbridge,[2] Hillingdon, Middlesex	Keith Park	South East England and London
12 Group	RAF Watnall,[3] Nottinghamshire	Trafford Leigh-Mallory	East Anglia, the Midlands, Mid Walesand North Wales
13 Group	RAF Newcastle,[4] Kenton Bar, Newcastle upon Tyne	Richard Saul	North of England and Scotland
14 Group	Drumossie Hotel, Inverness	Malcolm Henderson	Scotland

Sector	Group	Sector Station	Radio call sign	Satellite Airfield or airfields
A	11	Tangmere	SHORTJACK	Westhampnett
B	11	Kenley	SAPPER	Croydon
C	11	Biggin Hill	TOPHAT	West Malling, Gravesend[7]
D	11	Hornchurch	LUMBA	Gravesend, Rochford, Manston, Hawkinge
E	11	North Weald	COWSLIP	Stapleford Tawney, Martlesham Heath
F	11	Debden	GARTER	Martlesham Heath[8]
G	12	Duxford		Fowlmere
K	12	Wittering		Coltishall
L	12	Digby		Ternhill
M	12	Kirton-in-Lindsey		
N	12	Church Fenton		Leconfield

O	13	Usworth		Catterick
P	13	Acklington		
Q	13	Turnhouse		Drem, Grangemouth
R	13	Dyce		Grangemouth
S	13	Wick		Grimsetter, Sumburgh
W	10			Filton Boscombe Down, Colerne, Pembrey
Y	11	Middle Wallop	STARLIGHT	Boscombe Down, Warmwell, Exeter, some control overRNAS Roborough, St. Eval
Z	11	Northolt		Hendon

RAF Kenley

Squadron number	Date from/to	Equipped with
17	Until 19 August, moved to Tangmere	Hawker Hurricanes

3	Until 1940	Hawker Hurricanes
604	1940	Night fighters Bristol Blenheim and Beaufighters
229	1940	Hawker Hurricanes
64	1940	Supermarine Spitfires
66	1940	Supermarine Spitfires
616	1940 – 1942	Supermarine Spitfires
615	1937—1941	Hawker Hurricanes
253	1939—1941	Hawker Hurricanes
501	1940	Hawker Hurricanes

RAF Hornchurch.

Squadron Number	Dates from/to	Equipped with
41	1940—1941	Supermarine Spitfires
54	1939—1941	Supermarine Spitfires
65	1939—1940	Supermarine Spitfires
74	1939—1940	Supermarine Spitfires
222	1940—1944	Supermarine Spitfires
266	1940	Supermarine Spitfires
600	1940	Bristol Blenheim & Bristol Beaufighters MK1f
264	1940	Boulton Paul Defiants

Squadron	Dates	Equipped with
603	1940	Supermarine Spitfires
64	1940–1941	Supermarine Spitfires

No: 54 squadron were equipped with 4 variants of the Supermarine Spitfire, they were equipped with the (MK1), from 1939-1940, the (MK2a), and in 1941 the (MK. V a), and the (MK: V, b).

RAF North Weald.

Squadron Number	Dates From/To	Equipped with
1	1940 & 1944	Hawker Hurricanes
1(R.C.A.F)	1940	Hawker Hurricanes
25	1940	Bristol Blenheim
151	1940	Hawker Hurricanes
249	1940–1941	Hawker Hurricanes
257	1940	Hawker hurricanes
275	1940	Boulton Paul Defiants
419		Vikers Wellington

Squadron number 249 was a (gold coast) squadron.
Squadron number 257 was (Burma).
Squadron number 419 was a bomber squadron.

RAF Debden.

Squadron Number	Dates From/To	Equipped With

85	22 May 1940	Hawker Hurricanes
17	19 June 1940	Hawker Hurricanes
257	15 August 1940	Hawker Hurricanes
601	19 August 1940	Hawker Hurricanes
111	19 August 1940	Hawker Hurricanes
25	8 October 1940	Bristol Blenheim

RAF Middle Wallop.

Squadron Number	Dates From/To	Equipped With
236	July 1940	Bristol Blenheim
238	July 1940	Hawker Hurricanes
401(R.C.A.F.)	July 1940	Hawker Hurricanes
501	July 1940	Hawker Hurricanes
609	July 1940	Supermarine Spitfires
604	July 1940	Bristol Blenheim
222	August 1940	Supermarine Spitfires
238	September 1940	Hawker Hurricanes
23	September 1940	Bristol Blenheim

Squadron number 236 was a Light Bomber Squadron.

RAF Northolt.

Squadron Number	Dates From/ To	Equipped With
609	19 May 1940	Supermarine Spitfires
257	4 July 1940	Hawker Hurricanes
303	22 July 1940	Hawker Hurricanes
43	23 July 1940	Hawker Hurricanes
1	1 August 1940	Hawker Hurricanes
401	Mid-August 1940	Hawker Hurricanes
615	10 October 1940	Hawker Hurricanes
302	11 October 1940	Hawker Hurricanes

Above is the list of Airfield's of 11 group 1940

British Aircraft during the Battle of Britain

The most notable aircraft during the Battle of Britain was the Hawker Hurricane and the Supermarine Spitfire.

Hawker Hurricanes out-numbered the Supermarine Spitfires by 2-1 when war broke out. The Hawker Hurricane statistics were.

Hawker Hurricane mk.1

MK. 1

Engine: 1,030 HP (770 k w) Rolls-Royce Merlin mk. 2 or 3,

Armament: 8X, 303 inch (7.7mm) Browning Machine guns.

Length: 9.83m

Wingspan: 12m

Top speed: 547KPH (339MPH).

Supermarine Spitfire MK. 1 statistics were.

Engine: Rolls-Royce Merlin 2 or 3 1030 HP (770kw).

Armament: 4X .303 (7.7mm) Browning Machine guns.

Length: 9.12 m

Wingspan: 11.23m

Top speed: 557kph (346MPH).

Supermarine Spitfire mk.1

The most disappointing British fighter was the Boulton Paul Defiant. This aircraft was intended to be used as a "bomber destroyer".

Boulton Paul Defiant

Armament: 4X .303 (7.7mm) Browning Machine guns.

Length: 10.77m

Wingspan: 11.99m

Top speed: 489 kph (304 mph).

The reason this aircraft was disappointing was because, it was thought that the top speed of the modern bomber is so great, that it is only worthwhile to attack them under conditions which allow no relative motion between the fighter and its target, however the Defiant was found to be more effective as a night fighter, during the winter Blitz on London in 1940-41, defiants shot down more enemy aircraft than any other type.

The Bristol Blenheim was used by both Bomber and Fighter Command, 200 MK. 1 bombers were modified into MK. 1. f long range fighters, Engines 2X 840HP (630KW), Bristol Mercury VIII rapid piston engines.

Bristol Blenheim

Armament: .303in (7.7mm) Machine guns in the port wing, plus a .303in (7.7mm) Vickers k gun in the dorsal turret, Maximum bomb load 1,000lb 450Kg.

Length: 12.98m

Wingspan: 17.17m

Top speed: 428kmh (266mph).

The Blenheim was less nimble and slower than expected and by the end of June 1940 daylight Blenheim losses were to cause concern for fighter command, It was then decided that the 1f would be relegated mainly to night fighter duties where no 23 Squadron RAF who had already operated the type under night time conditions had better success.

Bristol Beaufighter

The Bristol Beaufighters entered service in early September 1940, at first, delivered in standard day fight camouflage schemes although the type was intended for night fighting roles the first night operations took place in September and October 1940, on the night of 19/ 20 November 1940 a Beaufighters 1. f equipped with A1 radar downed a JU88.

Bristol Beaufighters specifications were.
Engines: 2X 1,400 HP Bristol Hercules x1 fourteen cylinder air-cooled,
Armament, 4x 20mm Hispano cannon in nose and, 6x .303 inch Browning machines guns in wings.

Length: 12.60m

Wingspan: 17.62m

Top speed: 518kmh (321mph).

There were two variants of the Bristol Blenhiem in operation during the Battle of Britain, these were Blenheim MK. 1F with fighter command (night fighter) and Blenheim MK. 1VF with coastal command. There was a limited number of Westland Lysander in the opening days, 2 variants of the Hawker Hurricanes which were, MK1 and MK II a series 1, and 2 variants of the Supermarine Spitfire, the MK1 and MKII, both the Hawker Hurricane and the Supermarine Spitfire were with Fighter Command, who also had a limited number of Gloster Gladiator biplanes.

British Home Front

Gloster Gladiators statistics Crew: 1 Length: (8.3 m) Wingspan: (9.83 m) Height: 11 ft. 9 Wing area: 323 ft. Loaded weight: 4,594 lb (2,088 kg) Engine: 1 × Bristol Mercury IX radial engine, 830 HP (619 kW) Maximum speed: 407kmh 253 mph Cruise speed: 210 mph. The home guard or local defence volunteers was formed on 16 May 1940, a response to the secretary of state for war Anthony Eden's call for men of all ages who wish to do something for the defence of their country, 1,500 men rushed to join and they became a key part of the strategy of civilian mobilisation, convinced by the bleak international picture that a German invasion was on its way. In terms of mobilizing the greatest proportion of potential workers, maximizing output, assigning the right skills and the right tasks, and maintaining the morale and spirit of the people, much of this success was due to the systematic planned mobilization of women, as workers, soldiers and housewives. In mid-1940 the RAF (Royal

Air Force), was called on to fight the Battle of Britain, but it had suffered serious losses, it lost 458 aircraft, in France and was hard pressed. Throughout June and July 1940, ordinary people made preparations for the expected onslaught including the collection of scrap iron to make armaments and the construction of concrete pillboxes in suburban parks, women also played a crucial role on the home-front, fighting a daily battle of rationing, recycling, reusing, and cultivating food for m allotments and gardens.

The women had to work with rations that were given monthly.

ITEM	AMOUNT
Sweets	12oz every 4 weeks
Eggs	1 small every 4 weeks
Dried Eggs	1 packet every 4 weeks
Bacon & Ham	4oz
Meat	Approximately 1lb
Butter	4oz
Cheese	2oz-8oz
Tea	2oz
Sugar	12oz
Margarine	2oz
Milk	2-3 pints

Above is a ministry of food rationing list in 1942-1943, they had to take their ration books to regular shops for each items, who then stamp the book to say that it has been issued to the person.

The government decided to concentrate on only 5 types of aircraft in 1940, these were, Vikers Wellington, Armstrong Whitworth Whitley, Bristol Blenheim, Hawker Hurricane and Supermarine Spitfire. These aircraft received extraordinary priority covering the supply of material and equipment, labour was moved from other aircraft work to factories engaged on these specified types, the delivery of new fighters rose from 256 in April 1940 to 467 in September 1940, more than enough to cover their losses.

Food clothing petrol, leather and other such items were rationed, however items such as sweets (in 1940) and fruit were not rationed as they would spoil. Access to luxuries were severely restricted, although there was also a significant black market, families also grew victory gardens, and small home vegetable gardens to supply themselves with food.

The rationing system, which had been originally based on a specific basket of goods for each customer was much improved by switching to a point system which allowed the housewives to make choices based on their own priorities, people were especially pleased that rationing brought equality and the guarantee of a Decent meal at affordable cost, Air Raid Shelters, were built specifically to serve and protect against enemy air raids, however underground stations, tunnels, cellars, and basements in larger houses were suitable for safeguarding people during air raids. Such as Bounds Green underground.

Bounds Green station used as air raid shelter

A commonly used home shelter that was used was known as the Anderson Shelter which would be equipped with beds as refuge from air raids.

The Anderson shelter was designed in 1938 by William Patterson and Oscar Karl Kerrison in response to a request from the home office. They were designed to accommodate up to six persons, the main principle of protection was based on curved and straight galvanised corrugated steel panels, six curved panels were bolted together at the top, so forming the main body of the shelter, three straight sheets on each side, two more straight panels on each end, one containing the door making a total of 14 panels.

Anderson shelter in back yard for air raid protection

The shelters were 6ft high (1,8m), 4,5ft wide (1.4m), and 6.5ft (2.0m), long, they were buried 4ft (1.2m) deep in the ground and then covered with a minimum of 15inches (38cm) of soil above the roof. The earth banks could be planted with vegetables or flowers, the internal filling of the shelter was left to the owner so there were wide variations in comfort, Anderson shelters were issued free to all households that earned less than £ 5 per week (£ 270 in 2015), when adjusting inflation, those with a higher income were charged £ 7 (£ 380 in 2015) for the shelter. One and a half million shelters of this type were distributed between February 1939 and the outbreak of war.

Air-raid shelter Stalham Street 1940

In the united kingdom, it was being recognised early that public shelter in open spaces, especially near streets, were urgently needed for pedestrians, drivers and passengers in vehicles ECT. The program of building street command shelters commenced in March 1940. the government supplying the materials and being the moving force behind the scheme, and private builders executing the work under the supervision of surveyors, these shelters consisted of 14 inch brick walls and 1ft thick(0.30m) re-enforced concrete roofs similarly to but much thicker than the private shelters in back yards and gardens being introduced slightly later.

Many thousands of public air raid shelters were built for use on a communal basis they were sited on waste land, in parks and in the middle of wide public roads, they were not bomb proof and many people were killed by direct hits, but did offer protection from bomb blast, more people died from bomb blast than direct hit. The communal shelters were usually intended to accommodate around fifty persons, and were divided into various sections by interior walls with openings connecting the different sections, which were normally furnished with six bunks.

Cellars in the up were mainly included in larger houses and houses built up to the period of world war 1 after which detached and semi-detached properties were constructed without cellars, the lack of cellars in more recent houses became a major problem in the air raid precautions (A.R.P) programme in the u k during world war II. Basements also became available for the use of air-raid shelters, basements under, factories, schools, hospitals, department stores and other businesses were utilised.

However, the ad hoc shelters could bring additional dangers, as heavy machinery and materials or water storage facilities above the shelter. Plus insufficient support structures threatened to cause the collapse of basements. Railway arches, subways (underpasses) were also used for air raid protection at all times during world war II some tube stations and underground tunnels were used as night shelters, many other types of tunnels were also adapted for shelters to protect the civil population, some had had been built many years before, some had been part of an ancient defence system, some had even belonged to commercial enterprises such as coal mining.

The Victoria Tunnels at Newcastle upon Tyne for example, completed in 1842, used for transporting coal from collieries to the river Tyne, closed in 1860, and remained so till 1939, 12m in place the tunnels stretched in in parts beneath the city of Newcastle, were converted to air raid shelters with a capacity of 9,000 people, Tunnels built on the river Irwell in Manchester at the end of the 19thcentury were also used as air raid shelters, In Stockport, September 1938, 4 sets of underground tunnels were being dug in the red sand stone. The first set of shelters were opened on 28 October 1939, the smallest of the tunnels could accommodate 2,000 people and the largest 3,850 people, in South-east London, residents made use of Chistle Hurst caves, a 22 mile long series of tunnels, within a short time it became an underground city with some 15,000 inhabitants with electric lighting, a chapel and a hospital, one baby was born in the caves christened Rose Cavana Wakeman.

Air raid precautions

During the war, the A.R.P. was responsible for the issuing of gas masks, pre-fabricated air raid shelters such as (Anderson Shelters as well as Morrison Shelters), the upkeep of local public shelters, and the maintenance of the blackout. The A.R.P. also helped rescue people after air-raids and other attacks, some women became ARP ambulance attendants, whose job was to help administer first aid to casualties, search for survivors and in many grim instances, help recover bodies, sometimes those of their own colleagues.

An ARP warden would petrol the streets all night to look out for incendiary bombs being dropped and starting house fires whist the householders were away hiding in their shelters, also providing services such advice and training on how to wear gas masks, enforcing new laws such as The Blackout, warden post were set upon many street corners, meaning that people always knew where they could go for help. They had to supervise the blackout, and report people who continually ignored it to the police, they had to sound the air-raid sirens so that everyone knew to get to their shelters, also checking that everybody had their gas masks and they were fitted properly, as well as sounding alerts if there was a gas attack.

They also had to evacuate people away from unexploded bombs, and report the bombs and other damage to the warden control centre. The ARP wardens were trained in basic fire-fighting and first aid and could keep an emergency situation under control until official rescue services arrived. There were around 1.4 million ARP wardens in Britain during the war, almost all unpaid part-time volunteers who also held day jobs, initially, wardens were expected to be on duty three nights a week, but expectations were increased as the bombing grew worse. Although the standard procedures prescribed that the ideal warden would be at least 30 years old, men and women of all ages were wardens, Fire guard messengers.

With a general lack of radio communications and telephone communications prone to disruption by air-raids, many towns appointed child volunteers aged between 14-18 as messengers or runners, these fire guard messengers would run or cycle through the night raids ferrying messages between ARP's and the fire department units and incendiary volunteers with their bucket of sand.

5

The most famous German Aircraft of the battle Britain was the Messerschmitt BF109 e variant, a single seater single engine fighter, the BF109 an and the Spitfire were well matched in speed and agility.

BF109 specification was.

Engine: Daimler-Benz DB601 1,050hp direct fuel injection.

Armament: 2X MG FF cannon (60 rounds per gun), 2X 17.9mm MG machineguns (1000 rounds per gun)

Length: 8.64m

Wingspan: 9.87m Top speed: 348mph (56kmh)

BF109 E

At the start of the battle the Germans also used their twin engine Messerschmitt BF110 long range "destroyer" and was expected to engage in air to air combat while escorting the Luftwaffe bomber fleet, although the aircraft was well designed and the best of its class, being reasonably fast and possessing a respectable combat radius, the concept that the BF110 could defend bombers against a concerted attack by a force of fast single seated, single engine fighters was floored, when pitted against the Hurricane and Spitfire the BF110' s began to experience heavy losses through being only slightly more manoeuvrable than the bomber, they were meant to escort and suffering poor acceleration .

BF110

Engine: 2X Daimler-Benz DB 601 fuel injected

Armament: 2X MG FF cannon in nose of aircraft, 4X 7.9mm Machine gun (1000rpg). 1X 7.9mm Machine gun (750rpg).

Length: 12.07m

Wingspan: 16.25m

Top speed: 349mph (560kmh)

Type: Fighter escort/ Fighter Bomber.

JU 87 Stuka Dive Bomber

The Stuka dive bomber JU87 was specifically designed for dive bombing, the light bomb loads carried by the ju87 had been used to great effect during the Battle of France, However, the JU87 was slow and possessed an inadequate degree of defensive weaponry, furthermore, it could not be effectively protected by fighters, because of its low speed and the very low altitude at which it ended it dive bomb attacks, it was withdrawn from attacks on Britain in August after prohibitive losses.

The JU 88 was fitted with external dive brakes and a control system, similar to those of the JU87, and could carry out a dive bombing role although it was primarily used as a level bomber.

Junker JU88.
Engine: 2X Junkers Jumo 211b (1'200hp)
Armament: 6X 7.9mm Machine guns (2more lateral guns were added later)
Length: 47ft 1in
Wingspan: 59ft 10.3/ 4 in
Top speed: approximately 286mph
Type: medium range bomber.

During the Battle of Britain the JU88 remained unchanged, one of the most successful of the Luftwaffe raids was an attack on Portsmouth and the isle of white on 12 August 1940, and they were able to dive at high speed to evade contact with fighters.

Junker JU88

The Heinkel HE111 had done more damage during the Battle of Britain than any other German Plane, it had many variants, and the specification for the 'H' variant are as follows.

Heinkel HE11

Heinkel HE111.

Engines: 2X Junkers Jumo 211f 1350hp

Armament: 1X 12mm MG FF cannon, 1X 13mm MG131 machine gun, 7X 7.92mm MG 15 and/ or MG81 machine guns, 1X 4,409lb bomb (carried externally) and 1X 1,102lb bomb (carried internally) or 8X 551lb bombs (all carried internally).

Length: 16.40m
Wingspan: 22.60m
Top speed: 270mph (435kmh)
Type: long range medium bomber/ night bomber/ glider tug.

The third of the bombers that the Luftwaffe relied on is the Donier Do 17, its original aircraft had a pair of B M W engines and a top speed of 225mph and on the 5th version it was equipped with Hispano engines, the do 17 was mainly used as a night fighter.

Donier DO17Z Specifications.
Engines: 2X Bramo 323A 1.000hp radial engines.
Armament: 1X 20mm MG FF cannon (on some variants).
1X 13mm MG131 machine guns (on some variants).
6X 7.9mm MG15 and/ or MG81 machine guns.

Donier DO17

2,200lb bomb load (carried internally) or
1,100lb bomb load plus maximum fuel (all carried internally).
Length: 53ft 5inch
Wingspan: 59ft Top speed: 265mph

Type: Medium range medium bomber/ night bomber/ reconnaissance.
The Donier DO17Z was a much improved aircraft than the first DO17 that was made with more room for the nose gunner and a much better build design. One of the DO17Z variants was modified as a night fighter in late 1940 early 1941 and had nose section of a JU88c fitted with a cannon and machine gun, additional to that was the installation of an F.L.I.R (Forward Looking Infra-Red) detector. Said to be the world's first, the first success of the use of the F.L.I.R detector was the shooting down of a Vikers Wellington bomber of RAF bomber command on the night of October 16/ 17 1940 over the French-German border.

6

Winston Churchill, Born at Blenheim Palace, 30 November 1874 died 24 January 1965. (Aged 91). British Prime Minister from 1940 –1945 and again from 1951 to 1955. He was widely regarded as one of the greatest wartime leaders of the 20th century, he was also an Officer in the British Army, A historian, a writer and an artist, Churchill was the first person to be made an honorary Citizen of the United States.

Churchill was born into the aristocratic family of the dukes of Marlborough and branch of the spencer family, his father Lord Randolph Churchill was a charismatic politician, (tory), his mother Jennie Jarome was an

American socialite. As a young Army Officer he saw action in British India, the Sudan, and the Second Boer War.

He gained fame as a war correspondent and wrote books about his campaigns, at the outbreak of World War II on 3rd September 1939 Churchill was appointed first Lord of the admiralty and a member of the War Cabinet, when the board of the admiralty were informed they immediately sent a signal to fleet simply stating "Winston Is Back".

On 10 May 1040, following the resignation of the then Prime Minister Neville Chamberlain, Churchill was appointed as his replacement, his steadfast refusal to consider surrender helped inspire British resistance, especially during the difficult early days when the British commonwealth and empire stood alone in its active opposition to Adolf Hitler, Churchill was particularly noted for his speeches and radio broadcasts which helped inspire the British people, he was 65 years old when he took office. After his death on 24 January 1965 he was granted a State funeral one of the biggest in the history of Britain, 112 countries were represented inside St Pauls with only China refusing to send an envoy. 350 million people from across the globe watched the ceremony on television, including 25 million in Britain. After the ceremony Churchill was buried in his families plot at St Martin's church, Bladon Oxfordshire next to his mother and father.

Air chief marshal Hugh Dowding, born at St Ninian's Boy's preparatory school in Moffat Dumfriesshire Scotland on 24 April 1882 died 15 February 1970, the son of Arthur John Caswel Dowding and Maud Caroline Dowding (nee) Tremenheere. His father taught at Fettes College in Edinburgh before moving to the southern Scottish town of Moffat. Dowding attended St Ninian's as a boy, he continued his education at Winchester college at the age of 15, after 2 years of further schooling Dowding elected to pursue a military career and began classes at the royal military academy, Woolwich in September 1899, graduating the following year, he was commissioned as a second lieutenant and posted to the Royal Garrison Artillery on August 18 1900.

Promoted to lieutenant on May8 1902, he served with the Royal Garrison Artillery at Gibraltar, subsequently seeing service in Ceylon and Hong Kong before being posted to number7 Mountain Artillery Battery in India in 1904, after returning to the United Kingdom, he attended the Army staff college in 1912 before being promoted to captain on 18 August 1913 and being posted with the Royal Garrison Artillery on the Isle of white later that year. After becoming interested in aviation and visiting the aero club at Brooklands, he was able to convince them to give him flying lessons on credit. He was a quick learner and soon received his aviators Certificate, no: 711 on 19 December 1913, he then attended central flying school where he was awarded his wings although added to the reserve list of the Royal Flying Corps (RFC).

Dowding returned to the Isle of white to resume his duties with the Royal Garrison Artillery, however this arrangement was short lived and in August 1914 he joined the RFC as a pilot in no: 7 squadron, then transferred to no: 6 squadron in October 1914, and then, after two weeks as a Staff Officer in France, became a flight commander first with no: 9 squadron then with no: 6 squadron he was a British Officer in the Royal Air Force. He served as a fighter pilot and then as a commanding officer of 16 squadron during World War 1,

He became commanding officer (CO) of the wireless Experimental Establishment at Brooklands in March 1915, during the inter-war years he became Air officer commanding fighting area, Air Defence of Great Britain.

He then joined the air council, where he worked as a member for supply and research and later Air Member for research (1935).

In 1939 dowding was due to retire, he was asked to stay on until March 1940 Because of the tense international situation, he was only permitted to carry on through the Battle Of Britain, first until July and finally until November 1940. in 1940 he and his immediate superior Sir Cyril Newall then Chief of Air Staff resisted repeated requests from Winston Churchill to weaken the home defence by sending precious squadrons to France, on 24 November 1940, Dowding Gave his final message to the RAF, it reads.

> "my dear fighter boys, in sending you this my last message, I wish I could say all that is in my heart, I cannot hope to surpass the simple eloquence of the Prime Minister's words. 'Never before has so much been owed by so many to so few' the debt remains and will increase." In saying good bye to you I want you to know how continually you have been in my thoughts, and that though our direct connection may be severed, I may yet be able to help you in your gallant fight. Goodbye to you all, and god bless you all.

On 15 February 1970 he died in Tumbridge Wells and was buried in Westminster Abbey.

He proved instrumental in modernizing Britain's aerial defences, encouraging the design of advanced fighter aircraft. He was Air Officer Commanding RAF Fighter

Command during the Battle of Britain and is generally credited with playing a crucial role in Britain's defence, and hence, the defeat of Adult Hitler's plan to invade Britain.

Air Chief Marshal Keith Park. Born 15 June 1892 in Thames, New Zealand, the son of James Livingston, and Francis Livingston, his father was a Scottish professor, Park died 6 February 1975.

Keith Park was educated at kings college Auckland until 1906 and then at Otago Boy's High School in Dunedin where he served in the cadets, later he joined the Army as a Territorial Soldier in the New Zealand field artillery in 1911, at 19 years of age he went to sea as a purser aboard collier and passenger ships, earning the family nickname "skipper".

When the first world war broke out, park left the ships and joined his artillery Battalion, as a non-ranking officer, he participated in the landings at Gallipoli in April 1915, going ashore at Anzac Cove in the Trench warfare that followed, Park's achievements were recognized and in July 1915 he gained a commission as second lieutenant, he commanded an artillery Battalion during the August 1915 attack on Suvla Bay and endured more months of squalor in the trenches. It was then that park took the unusual decision to transfer from the New Zealand Army to the British Army, joining the Royal Horse and field Artillery. He joined the Royal Flying Corps (RFC) in December 1916.

Between the wars Keith Park was to pass through the RAF Staff College, become the Air attaché, in Buenos Aires, he was a commanding officer at one of Britain's peacetime fighter stations, prior to 1940 he was appointed Senior Air Staff Officer to Hugh Dowding, where together they built a bond where they gained the greatest respect for each other. At the beginning of the war, when fighter command was divided up into groups Dowding had no hesitation in placing Keith Park C-in-C of 11 group, the most important group in Fighter Command.

On 20 December 1946, Park retired and was promoted to Air Chief Marshal, and returned to New Zealand, where he took up a number of civic roles and was elected to the Auckland city council. While it was Sir Hugh Dowding that controlled the battle from day to day, it was Keith Park who controlled it hour by hour. Keith Park lived in New Zealand until his death on 6 February 1975.

Air Chief Marshal Trafford Leigh-Mallory.

Born July 1892 in Cheshire his father Herbert Leigh-Mallory was a vicar and his brother was the mountaineer George Leigh-Mallory. Trafford Leigh-Mallory died 14 November 1944,

He was a senior commander in the Royal Air Force,

Leigh-Mallory served as a Royal Flying Corps pilot and squadron commander during World War 1, remaining in the newly formed RAF after the war. Leigh-Mallory served in a variety of staff and training appointments throughout the 1920' s and 30' s.

He was educated at Haileybury and after this went to Magdalene college, Cambridge, it was at Cambridge that he met Arthur Tedder, the future marshal of the RAF Leigh-Mallory gained a degree in law and planned to be a barrister, the outbreak of WWI was to change his plans,

When WWI started Leigh-Mallory immediately volunteered to join a Territorial Force battalion of the king's Liverpool regiment as a private, he was commissioned as a second lieutenant on 3 October 1914, then transferred to the Lancashire fusiliers though officer training kept him in England when his battalion embarked, in the spring of 1915, he went to the front with the south Lancashire regiment and was wounded during the attack at the, second battle of Ypres. He was promoted to lieutenant on 21June 1915, after his recovery he joined the Royal Flying Corps, and on July 7 1916 he was posted as a lieutenant in the RFC to no: 7 squadron.

After WWI Leigh-Mallory thought about re-entering the law profession, but with little prospect of a law career, he stayed in the recently formed Royal Air Force (RAF) with a promotion to Major on 1 August 1919. (Rank renamed Squadron Leader from the same date) and took command of the armistice Squadron.

Leigh-Mallory took command of 12 group and proved

an energetic organiser and leader, on 1 November 1938 he was promoted to Air Vice Marshal, one of the younger AVM's then serving in the RAF, he was greatly liked by his staff, but his relations with his airfield station commanders were strained. During the Battle of Britain Leigh-Mallory quarrelled with vice air marshal Keith Park, the commander of 11 group, Park who was responsible for the defence of south east England and London, had stated that 12 group was not doing enough to protect the air fields in the south east. Leigh-Mallory on the other hand, had devised with acting Squadron Leader Douglas Bader a massed fighter formation known as the Big Wing, which they used, with little success, to hunt German bomber formations, Hugh Dowding, Head of fighter command believed that not enough was being done to allow Wing-sized formations to operate successfully.

He worked energetically in political circles to bring about the removal of Park from command of 11 group, after the Battle of Britain, Air Chief Marshal Charles Portal, the new chief of air staff, who had agreed with Leigh-Mallory, removed both Park and Dowding in december1940. Leigh-Mallory was then appointed command of 11 group because he was seen as an offensive minded leader. He was promoted to acting Air Marshal in July 1942, then in November 42 replaced Sholto Douglas as head of fighter command, and was promoted to the temporary rank of Air Marshal on 1 December 1942.

On August 16 1944 with the Battle of Normandy almost over, Leigh-Mallory was appointed Air Commander-in-

Chief of South Asia command with the temporary rank of Air Chief Marshal, but before he could take up his post he and his wife were killed on route to Burma when Avro York mw 126 in which they were flying, crashed into the French alps killing all on board.

Vice Air Marshal Sir Christopher Quintin Brand. Born 25 May 1893 died 7 March 1968. He was born in Beaconsfield South Africa (now part of Kimberly, Northern Cape). The son of a C.I.D Inspector in the Johannesburg police.

He joined the South African Defence Force in 1913, during the years 1914-1915 Brand continued to serve in the Union Defence Force. In 1915 Brand came to England and transferred to the Royal Aero Club, He was a pioneer aviator and served with distinction in the Royal Flying Corps and the Royal Air Force in WWI. In February 1918, he became commander of 112 Squadron, A home defence night fighter squadron equipped with specially modified Sopwith Camels, flying from Throwley in Kent. He was then appointed commander of 151 Squadron RAF at Fontaine-sur-Maye in France, a night fighter squadron formed to combat German night raids over the western front, the squadron downed 26 German aircraft with Brand himself shooting down four, Brand claimed 12 victories in 1917 and 1918, seven victories with no: 1 squadron, four with 151 squadron and one with 112 squadron, and was awarded the distinguished Flying Cross during this period.

During the Second World War Brand was Air Officer commanding no: 10 fighter group. (10 fighter battle group) responsible for the defence of south-west England and South Wales, Brand actively supported Air Vice Marshal Keith Park, in advocating the use of small, rapidly deployed, groups of fighters to intercept the Luftwaffe raiders, as the pressure on Britain eased he was appointed the head of no: 20 (training) group.

Brand died in Southern Rhodesia on 7 March 1968.

Vice Air Marshal Richard Ernest Saul. Born in Dublin Ireland in 1891, at the start of WWI he was a second lieutenant in the Royal Army Service Corp but by 1916 he was flying officer (observer) with no: 16 squadron of the army's Royal Flying Corps, during the war he rose to command no: 4 squadron and after the armistice he commanded no: 7 squadron and then 12 squadron.

In 1925 he was given command of no: 2 squadron, a keen sportsman Saul played rugby for the RAF. In March 1939 no: 13 group war reformed to defend Northern Ireland and Scotland including the strategically important naval base at Scapa Flow. Richard Saul took over command in the summer.

From 1940 he was Air Officer commanding 12 group and the Air Officer commanding Air Defences Eastern Mediterranean from 1943. Saul retired from the RAF on 29 June 1944 and then served as the chairman of the United Nations Relief and Rehabilitation Administrations mission in the Balkans, Richard Saul Died on 30 November 1965, two days after being hit by a car.

William Lyon Mackenzie King. Was the dominant Canadian political leader from the 1920' s through to the 1940' s, with twenty-two years in office he was the serving prime minister in Canadian history,

He was born in Berlin Ontario (now known as Kitchener) to John King and Isabelle grace Mackenzie on 17 December 1874, his maternal grandfather was William Lyon Mackenzie, the first mayor of Toronto and leader of the Upper Canada rebellion in 1837, and his father was a lawyer, later a professor at Osgoode hall law school. His father was a lawyer with a struggling practice in a small city, and never enjoyed financial security.

King earned five university degrees, he obtained three degrees from the university of Toronto, B.A 1895, LL.B 1896, and the M.A 1897, he earned his LL.B in 1896 from Osgoode Hall Law school, in March 1936 in response to the German remilitarization of the Rhineland, King had the Canadian high commissioner in London inform the British government that if Britain want to war with Germany over the Rhineland issue that Canada would remain neutral. In June 1937, during an imperial conference of all the dominion prime ministers in London convened during the Coronation of King George VI and Queen Elizabeth, King informed British prime minister Neville Chamberlain that Canada would only go to war if Britain were directly attacked, but if Britain became involved in a continental war then chamberlain was not to expect Canada's support.

Also in 1937 King visited Germany and met with Hitler, becoming the only North American head to do so, he infamously described Hitler as harmless and peaceful. King realised the likelihood of WWII before Hitler invaded Poland in 1939 and began mobilizing on August 25 1939, with full mobilization on September 1 1939, the prime minister waited until 10 September, a full week after the war declaration by King George VI, when a vote in the house of commons could take place to support the government's decision to declare war.

King and Canada were largely ignored by Winston Churchill, despite Canada's major role in supplying food, raw materials, munitions and money to the hard pressed British economy, training airmen for the commonwealth, guarding the western half of the North Atlantic Ocean against German U-boats. To re-arm Canada he built the Royal Canadian Air Force as a visible military power, while at the same time keeping it separate from Britain's Royal Air Force.

He was instrumental in obtaining the British Commonwealth Air Training plan Agreement which was signed in December 1939, binding Canada, Britain, New Zealand and Australia to a program that eventually trained half of the airmen from those four nations in the Second World War.

King died from pneumonia at Kingsmere on July22 1950.

Air Chief Marshal Lloyd Samuel Breadner. Born 14July 1894 Carlton place, Ontario, his father was Samuel Marsh Breadner, and mother was Caroline Alberta (Watkins) Breadner, Lloyd Breadner was a Canadian military pilot, he obtained his pilots certificate at wright flying school and was commissioned in the British Royal Navy Air Service on 28 December 1915 during WWI he served on the western front as a fighter pilot in the no: 3 (naval) squadron, and promoted to flight lieutenant (RNAS) on 31 December 1916.

He was awarded the Distinguished Service Cross, on May 23 1917, released from the RAF with the rank of Major in March 1919. He was commissioned, promoted to squadron leader in 1920 and transferred to the Royal Canadian Air Force (RCAF) on its formation in 1924. He became controller of civil Aviation in 1922, and later commanded Camp Borden from January 15 1924 to September 23 1925, he was promoted on 1 April 1924 to the rank Wing Commander, after attending RAF Staff College he was promoted to group captain on 1 February 1936 and to Air Commodore on May 29 1940. He was promoted to Air Marshal on November 19 1941 then Air Officer, commandeering-chief RCAF overseas in January 1944.

Breadner was promoted on his retirement on November 25 1945 to Air Chief Marshal, the first Canadian to hold this rank. Breadner died in a Boston, Massachusetts hospital after suffering from ill health on 14 March 1952.

All together during the Battle of Britain, the British/Canadian servicemen/women casualties and or losses were.

544 Aircrew Killed. 422 Aircrew Wounded.

1,547 Aircraft destroyed.

There were also losses in the WAAF and civilian losses estimated at 40,000, and 20,000 were in London.

The WAAF Women's Auxiliary Air Force proved there metal, working with bombs bursting nearby during the bombings.

German Commanders and Leaders

Adolf Hitler. In German (Adolf Hitler). Born on 20 April 1889 in Branau Am Inn, a town in Austria-Hungary (in present Austria), close to the border with the German Empire. He was the fourth of six children to Alois Hitler and Klara polzl. When Hitler was three, the family moved to Passau Germany. Hitler did not do particularly well in school, leaving formal education in 1905, unable to settle in to a regular job.

When Hitler was eight he took singing lessons, sang in a church choir and even considered becoming a priest. In

1900 his brother Edmund died from measles which deeply affected him and he was younger than Hitler, he changed from a confident, outgoing, and conscientious student to a morose, detached, sullen boy who constantly fought with his father and teachers.

Like many Austrian Germans, Hitler began to develop German nationalist ideas from a young age, he wished to become an artist but was rejected by the academy in Vienna, but showed great intellectual potential at primary school and was extremely popular as well as being admired for his leadership qualities, however, secondary school was tougher and Hitler stopped trying.

He expressed loyalty only to Germany, Hitler and his friends used the greeting "Hail" and the song "Deutschland lied" instead of the Austrian imperial anthem. After his father's death on 3 January 1903 Hitler's performance at school deteriorated and his mother allowed him to leave, he enrolled at the Realschule in Steyl in September 1904, where his behaviour and performance showed some improvement, in 1905 after passing a repeat final exam, Hitler left the school without any ambitions for a further education or clear plan for a career.

At the age of 18 he moved to Vienna with money he inherited after his death, in order to pursue in art, as this was his best subject at school. However his applications for both the Vienna academy of art and the school of architecture were rejected.

During the First World War he volunteered to fight for the German army and gained the rank of corporal earning accolades as a dispatch-runner. He won several awards for bravery, including the iron cross first class, he spent nearly half his time behind enemy lines, he was present at the first battle of Ypres, the battle of the Somme, the battle of Arras and the battle of Passchendaele, and was wounded at the Somme, He was decorated for bravery receiving the iron cross second class in 1914, he served in the Bavarian army and posted to the Bavarian Reserve Infantry Regiment 16 (1st company of the last regiment). On a recommendation by Lieutenant Hugo Guttmann, Hitler's Jewish superior he received the iron cross first class on August 4 1918.

After the war he returned to Munich, he remained in the army and discharged from the army on 30 March 1920. By the 1930' s the Nazi's were polling around 6.5 million votes, in the presidential elections Hitler came second. On 30 January 1933, president Hindenburg was forced to appoint Hitler as chancellor, given his popular support, in office Hitler set about consolidating his power appointing Nazi's to government and gaining control of emergency power, he eliminated all opposition, in the name of emergency control, and with the death of Hindenburg in 1934, Hitler's power was secured, he was made Fuhrer und Reichskanzier (leader and chancellor).

As head of state Hitler became supreme commander of the armed forces. The traditional loyalty oath of servicemen was altered to affirm loyalty to Hitler personally. Rather than the office of supreme commander or the state. On August 19 the merger of the presidency with the chancellorship was approved by 90% of the electorate voting in a Plebiscite.

Hitler began a military build-up on Germany's western front in April 1940, German Forces invaded Denmark and Norway. On 9 April Hitler proclaimed the birth of the Greater Germanic Reich. His vision of a united empire of the Germanic nations of Europe where the Dutch, Flemish, and Scandinavians were joined into a "radically pure "policy under German leadership.

Hitler made peace overtures to the new British Prime Minister Winston Churchill, and upon their rejection he ordered a series of aerial attacks on the Royal Air Force airbases and radar stations in south east England. The German Luftwaffe failed to defeat the RAF. There has been many theories of whether he was shot and killed or committed suicide or escaped and lived in a different country, the version that I am putting down is that. Hitler died April 30 1945 from a gunshot to the side of the head (suicide) and his wife died the same day from poison.

Wilhelm Bodewin Johann Gustav Keitel. Born in the village of Helmschero de near Gandersheim in the Duchy of Brunswick on 22 September 1882, The eldest son of carl Keitel and Apollonia Vissering, after completing his education at gymnasium in Gottingen, he planned to take over his family's estates, his father resisted, instead he embarked on a military career in 1901.

Becoming an officer cadet of the Prussian army. As a commoner he did not join the cavalry but the mounted 46th lower-Saxon field Artillery regiment in Walfenuttel serving as Adjutant from 1908. On 18 April 1909, Keitel married Lisa Fontaine, they had six children, one died in infancy, during WWI, Keitel served on the western front with his artillery regiment and took part in the fighting in Flanders, where he was severely wounded in his right forearm by a shell fragment. Elevated to the rank of Captain, Keitel quickly recovered, and was posted to the general staff of the 19th Reserve infantry division in 1915. He stayed in what was the German army after the war ended and initially served as a divisional general staff officer, for two years, Keitel also taught at the Hanover Cavalry School.

He also fought in the first battle of the Marne, battle of Verdan and the battle of pesschendaele, being awarded the iron cross second class and first class. After the war the army was limited to only 100,000 soldiers. In 1937 Keitel was promoted to the rank of full general (generaloberst) in the following year, after the Bloomberg-Fritsch affair, the war ministry was replaced by the supreme command of the armed forces and Keitel was appointed as its chief. This effectively made him Germany's war minister and accordingly, he was appointed to the Hitler cabinet. He would have been instrumental in the planning for the polish invasion in September 1939.

The success of this attack, and the success of the attack on western Europe in 1940 > resulted in Hitler promoting Keitel to field marshal in 1940, he advised Hitler against invading France and opposed operation Barbarossa, both times he backed down in the face of Hitler and tendered his resignation, which Hitler refused to accept. Keitel realized the Germans would be unable to win the Battle of Britain, as the British had the backing of the almost unlimited resources of the United States.

After Hitler's death on 3 April 1945, Keitel stayed on as a

member of the short –lived Flensburg government under grand admiral Karl Donitz upon arriving in Flensburg Alber Speer found Keitel to be grovelling to Donitz in the same way he had grovelled to Hitler. During the Battle of Berlin Keitel called for counterattacks to drive back the soviet forces and relieve Berlin, however, there were insufficient German forces to carry out such attacks. On 8 May 1945, Donitz authorised Keitel to sign an uncomfortable surrender in Berlin. Although Germany had surrendered to the allies a day earlier Stalin had insisted on a second surrender ceremony in Berlin. On May 13 1945, he was arrested and charged with crimes against humanity and conspiring to commit crimes against peace. Keitel went on trial at the Nuremburg trials in 1946 where he claimed that he was simply following orders as any good soldier would. The claim was rejected and he was found guilty on all charges and sentenced to death, he was found guilty of criminal offences as opposed to military ones. That is why his request to be shot was rejected and why he was hung on October 16 1946, a punishment fit for a criminal as opposed to a soldier.

Herman Goring (or **Goering**). Born in Bavaria on 12 January 1893, his father was a member of the colonial service in Africa, Goring found fame in WWI as a fighter ace. He won numerous awards for bravery and was the last commander of the legendary Richthofen fighter squadron.

Goring was the Fourth of five children, at sixteen he was sent to military school where he graduated with distinction, he joined the Prince Wilhelm Regiment (112th infantry) of the Prussian army in 1912. When WWI began in August 1914, goring was stationed at Mulhouse with his regiment, a garrison town only a mile from the French Frontier. He was hospitalized with rheumatism as a result of the damp of the trench warfare. While recovering in hospital his friend Bruno Loerzer convinced him to transfer to what would have become, By October 1916, the luftstreikrafte, (air combat force) of the German army, but his request was turned down, later that year goring flew as Loerzers observer fieldflieger abteilung 25 (FF25), goring had informally transferred himself,

He was discovered and sentenced to three weeks confined to barrack, but by the time it was imposed Goring's association with loerzer had been made official. They were assigned as a team to FF25, in the Crown Prince's fifth army where they flew reconnaissance and bombing missions, for which the crown prince invested both Goring and Loerzer with the iron cross first class. On 7 July 1918, following the death of Wilhelm Reinhard, successor to Manfred Von Richthofen. Goring was made commander of the formed "flying circus", Jagdgeschwader 1, his arrogance made him unpopular with the men in his squadron.

In the last days of WWI he was repeatedly ordered to withdraw his squadron, and at one point to surrender the aircraft to the allies, but he refused, many of his pilots deliberately crash-landed their planes to keep them from falling into enemy hands. Goring joined the Nazi party in 1923 after hearing a speech from Hitler. He was given command of the Sturmabteilung (SA) as the Oberster

SA-Fuhrer in 1923. on September 3 1939 the UK declared war on Germany after they invaded Poland, Goring had already announced in a radio speech, "if as much as a single enemy aircraft flies over German soil, my name is Meier," something that would return to haunt him when the RAF began bombing German Cities on 11 May 1940, his power started to wane after the failure of the Luftwaffe to destroy fighter command during the battle of Britain, He was confident that the Luftwaffe could defeat the RAF within days.

Goring, like Admiral Erich Reader. Commander in chief of the Kriegsmarine (Navy), was pessimistic about the chance of success of the planned operation (codenamed operation sea-lion). Goring hoped that a victory in the air would be enough to force peace without an invasion, the campaign failed and the planned operation was postponed indefinitely on 17 September 1940. Goring was named as Hitler's successor in 1941 and it stated that, if Hitler lost his freedom of action Goring had complete authority to act on his behalf as his deputy. By 26 April1940 goring was moved to Hitler's castle at Mauterndorf, in his will and testament, Hitler expelled Goring from the party and rescinded the decree making him his successor, he was taken into custody near Radstadt on 6 May 1945 by elements of the 36th infantry division of the United States army. This move saved his life as Bormann had ordered him executed if Berlin had fallen. Goring was the second highest ranking Nazi official to be tried at Nuremburg. The prosecution levelled an indictment of four charges, including a charge of conspiracy, waging war of aggression, war crimes, including the plundering and removal to Germany of works of art and other property, and crimes against humanity, including the disappearance of political and other opponents under the Nacht und Nebal (night and fog) decree. The torture and ill treatment of prisoners of war, and the murder and enslavement of civilians, including what was at the time Estimated to be 5,700,000 Jews, not permitted to make a lengthy statement Goring declared himself to be "in the sense of the indictment not guilty". Goring was due to be hung on October 16 1946, but just hours before his execution, he committed suicide in his cell by taking cyanide, on 15 October 1946.

Albert Kesselring. Born in Marksteft Bavaria on 20 November 1885 to Carl Adolf Kesselring a school master and town councillor and Rosina, who was Carl's second cousin. In 1904 joined the German army as a Fahnenjunker (Officer Cadet) in the 2nd Bavarian foot artillery regiment. The regiment was based at Metz and was responsible for maintaining it forts.

He remained with the regiment until 1915 except for

periods at the military academy from 1905 to 1906. He was commissioned as a lieutenant (leutnant) when he had concluded, and at the school of artillery and engineering in Munich from 1909 to 1910.

In 1912 Kesselring completed training as a balloon observer in a dirigible section– an early sign of an interest in aviation. During WWI Kesselring served with his regiment in Lorraine until the end of 1914, when he was transferred to the 1st Bavarian foot artillery, which formed part of the sixth army, on 19 May 1916, he was promoted to Houptmann (Captain). In 1916 he was transferred again to the 3rd Bavarian foot artillery, he distinguished himself in the battle of Arras using his tactical acumen to halt a British advance, for his services on the western front, he was decorated with the iron cross 2nd class and 1st class. In 1917 he was posted to the general staff, despite not attending the Bavarian war academy, he served on the eastern front on the staff of the 1st Bavarian Landwehr division, in January 1918 he returned to the western front as an officer with the II and III Bavarian corps.

From 1919 to 1922, Kesselring served as a Battery commander with the 24th artillery regiment he joined the Reichswehr on October 1st 1922 and was posted to the military training at the reichswehr ministry in Berlin, he remained at this post until 1929. In his time with the ministry he was involved in organising the army, trimming staff overheads to produce the best possible army, he helped reorganize the ordinance department, laying the ground work for the research and development efforts that would produce new weapons.

On 1 October 1933, Kesselring was discharged from the army against his wishes, and put in charge of the administration office, the forerunner of the Reich air ministry with the rank of oberst (Colonel). At 48 years old he learned to fly, he believed that first-hand knowledge of all aspects of aviation was crucial to being able to command airmen. In the polish campaign that began WWII, Kesselring's Luftwaffe 1 operated in support of army group north, Kesselring strove to provide the best possible close air support to the ground forces. He attempted to cut the polish communication by making a series of air attacks against Warsaw. Kesselring himself was shot down over Poland by the polish air force. For his part in the polish campaign, Adolf Hitler personally awarded him the knights cross of the iron cross, Kesselring's Luftwaffe 1 was not involved in the preparations for the campaigns in the west, instead it remained in the east on garrison duty, establishing new airbases and an air raid precautions network in occupied Poland.

Goring appointed Kesselring the commander of Luftwaffe 2, after relieving Helmuth Felmy, on 12 January 1940, Kesselring flew to his new headquarters in Munster the next day, he brought his own chief of staff, as Fely's chief of staff was also relieved, he led the operations of air fleet II over France, in the air support over Dunkirk and finally in the battle of Britain, on 30 June 1940 he was promoted to air marshal. In September 1941 he was transferred to Rome as commander in chief South, he was supreme commander in Italy and the Mediterranean in September 1943, then from 1943 to 1945 directed the steady retreat of the German army's under the onslaught of the allied troops and Italian partisans,. From March 1 1945 he headed Hitler's last Stand on the Rhine. On May 7 he surrendered the Southern half of the German Forces to the Americans.

Kesselring himself surrendered to an American major at Saalfelden. Kesselring was hoping to be able to make a start on the rehabilitation of Germany, but found himself placed under arrest on 15 May 1945, he was held in a number of American prisoner of war (P.O.W) camps before being transferred to British custody in 1946. he testified at the Nuremburg trials of Hermann Goring, but his offers to testify against soviet, American, and British commanders were declined, Kesselring was tried by a British military court in Venice in May 1947 and was sentenced to death for the shooting of the 335 Italian hostages, (Ardeparin Caves Massacre) in March 1944, in October 1947 the sentence was commuted to life imprisonment, because the British Prime Minister, Field Marshal Alexander, now governor general of Canada sent a telegram to prime minister Clement Attlee in which they expressed his hopes that Kesselring's sentence would be commuted, "he state that we have no complaints against him, Kesselring and his soldiers fought against us hard but clean" Winston Churchill branded it as too harsh, in October 1952 he was released for reasons of ill health, he died in badnauheim on 16 July 1960.

Hugo Sperrle. Born in Ludwigsburg on 7 February 1885, his father was a brewer, he joined the German army in 1903 and was Commissioned as lieutenant, later promoted to obeleutnant, after the outbreak of WWI, he transferred to the Luftstreikrafte (German army air service) serving as an observer in a two-seater aircraft. During the war he rose through the ranks and at its conclusion was commander of the air components of the German 7th army, he earned the iron cross award in 1914, After WWI he became a member of the para-military Freikorps in the 20's he commanded the secret German school in the Soviet Union, before re-joining the reichswehr since Germany was not allowed to create aerial units, he served in logistics and army command positions, after the Nazi's took over, a new air force, the Luftwaffe was established, Sperrle immediately joined and was given the rank of major General, in 1936 he went to Spain as head of the Condor Legion,

The condor legion was initially equipped with around 100 aircraft and 5,136 men. Sperrle demanded higher performance aircraft from Germany and eventually received the Heinkel HE111, Junkers Stuka dive bombers and the Messerschmitt BF109, in October 1937 he returned to Nazi Germany to become commander of Air Fleet 3, this unit saw no action during the Poland campaign, but was committed from May onwards in France, playing an important role as tactical bombing support unit, during the 1940 field marshal ceremony he was made a general field marshal, of the Luftwaffe. Air fleet 3, stationed in France North, played a major role in the Battle of Britain, from June till October 1940 and The Blitz, to May 1941, Sperrle played an important role in the blitzkrieg tactics used during the western offensive.

He remained in France and in May 1941 he became Air commander in the west, however, he was unable to stop the allied landing in Normandy in June 1944, two months later he was dismissed from office, by the time of the D-day landings June 6 1944 the Luftwaffe could muster only some 319 operational aircraft over the landing beaches to hold back an invading air armada of almost 10,000 planes of all types. Field marshal Sperrle was captured by the allies and charged with war crimes in the High Command Trial at the Nuremburg trials but was acquitted. After the war. He lived quietly and died in Munich on 2 April 1953, aged 68.

Benito Mussolini. Born in Dovia di Predappio, a small town in the province of Forli in Emilia-Romagna on 29 July 1883. His father Alessandro Mussolini was a blacksmith and a socialist while his mother Rosa Mussolini (nee Maltoni) was a devoutly catholic school teacher, owing to his father's political learnings, Mussolini was named after Mexican reformist President Benito Juarez.

As a young boy Mussolini would spend some time helping his father and his smithy. He showed much intelligence as a youth, but was boisterous and disobedient. His father installed into him a passion for socialist politics and a defence against authority, in 1901 at 18 years old he took his diploma di maestro and taught secondary school briefly. He voluntarily exiled himself to Switzerland (1902 to 1904) he formed a dilettante's culture notably only for its philistinism, not surprisingly

Mussolini based it on Friedrich Nietzsche, George Sorel, and Max Stimer, his move to Switzerland was partly to avoid military service. He worked as a stone smith in Geneva Fribourg and Bern but was unable to find a permanent job. Mussolini became active in the Italian socialist movement in Switzerland, working for the paper "L'avvernie del Lavoratore, organising meetings, giving speeches to workers and serving as secretary of the Italian workers union in Lausanne. In 1903 he was arrested by the Bernese police because of the advocacy of a violent general strike, and spent two weeks in jail. Mussolini returned to Italy on 1904, rendered military service, and engaged in politics full time thereafter.

He became a member of the socialist party in 1900 and his politics, like his culture was exquisitely bohemian Mussolini joined the army on 30 December 1904, he joined the corps of the bersaglieri in Fotli in February 1909, Mussolini left Italy once again this time to take up the job as the secretary of the labour party in the Italian-speaking city of Trento, which at the time was part of Austria-Hungary, he also did office work for the local Socialist party, and edited to it newspaper, returning to Italy he spent a brief tome in Milan, and then in 1910, he returned to his home town of Farli, where he edited the weekly lotta di classe (the class struggle).

With the outbreak of WWI a number of socialist parties initially supported the war when it began in August1914, once the war had begun Austrian, British, French German and Russian socialist followed the rising nationalist current by supporting the country's intervention in the war. Mussolini initially held official support for the party's decision in an August 1914 article Mussolini wrote, "Down with the war we remain neutral." He saw the war as an opportunity, both for his own ambitions as well as those of socialists and Italians. He was influenced by anti-Austrian Italian nationalist sentiment believing that the war offered Italians in Austria-Hungary the chance to liberate themselves from the rule of the Habsburgs, he eventually decided to declare support for the war by appealing to the need to overthrow the Hohenzollern and Hapsburg monarchies in Germany and Austria-Hungary who he had claimed had constantly repressed socialism.

From 1936 to 1939. Mussolini provided huge amounts of military support to the nationalists in the Spanish civil war, this active intervention on the side of Franco further distanced Italy from France and Britain. As a result Mussolini's relationship with Adolf Hitler became closer and he chose to accept the German Annexation of Austria in 1938. by the late 1930' s Mussolini's obsession with dermatology led him to conclude that Britain and France were finished as powers, and that it was Germany and Italy who were destined to rule Europe if for other reason than there demographic strength. He believed that an alliance with Germany was preferable to an alignment with Britain and France, as it was better to be allied with the strong instead of the weak. As WWII began caino and Viscount Halifax were holding secret phone conversation the British wanted Italy on their side against Germany as it had been in WWI. In September 1940, the Italian tenth army commanded by Randolfo Graziani crossed from Italian Libya into Egypt where British forces were located, during 25 October1940 sent the Italian air corps to Belgium, where the air force took part in the Battle of Britain for around two months, on 24 July 1943 he was summoned to The royal palace by king Emmanuel III who had planned to oust Mussolini earlier, when Mussolini tried to tell the King about the meeting, Victor Emmanuel cut him off and told him he was being replaced.

After Mussolini left the palace, he was arrested by Carabinieri on the kings orders on 13 October Italy declared war on Germany, thousands of troops were supplied to fight the Germans. Two months after Mussolini had been dismissed and arrested, he was rescued from prison by Germany. Three days after his rescue Mussolini was taken to Germany for a meeting with Hitler. 28 April 1945 Mussolini was shot in Mezzegra.

OPERATIONS DURING BATTLE OF BRITAIN.

The Germans plan for a land invasion of England in 1940 was codenamed (Operation Sea Lion). This is the order of Battle for the modified German plan in August 1940.

German forces consisted of.

Heeresgrouppe A. commanded by General field marshal Gerd Von Rundstedt.

16. Armee— generaloberst Ernst Busch (First wave)

XIII. Armee-Korps— General Heinrich Gottfried von Vietinghoff Gennant scheel

17 infanterie division

35 infanterie division

Luftwaffe 2/ Flak regiment 14

VII. Armee Korps Generabberst, Eugen Rittler Von Schobert

1 gebirgs division

7 infanterie division

Luftwaffe 1/ Flak regiment 26

Second wave

V Armee korps— general Richard Rouff

12 infanterie division.

30 infanterie division

XXXI. Armee Korps general de Panzertrupen. Georg-Hans Rein Hardt

8 Panzer– division

10 Panzer-division

29 infanterie division (MOT) infanterie division (MOT)

grabdeutschland.

Infanterie division liebstandarte SS Adolf Hitler (MOT).

Third wave.

IV. Armee Korps general Viktor Von Schwedler

24 infanterie division

58 infanterie division

XXXII Armee korps general Walter Kuntze

45 infanterie division

164 infanterie division

9 Armee generaloberst Adolf Stouss.

First wave...

XXXVIII Armee Korps general Erich Von Monstein

26 infanterie division

34 infanterie division

VIII. Armee Korps general Walter Heitz.

6 Gebirgs division.

8 infanterie division

28 infanterie division

Second wave.

XV. Armee Korps Generoberst Hermann Hoth

4 Panzer Division

7 Panzer Division

20 infanterie division (MOT).

Third wave.

XXIV Armee Korps General Leo Freiherr Von Schweppengburg.

15 infanterie division

78 infanterie division

Heeres groupe c commanded by general field marshal Wilhelm Ritter Von Leeb.

6 Armee General field marshal Walther Von Reichenau.

1 Armee Korps General Walter Graf von Brockdorf Ahleldt

6 infanterie division

256 infanterie division

Airborne Formations General Kurt Student.

7 Flieger division

22 infanterie division (Luftlande)

Ball Lehr Regiment Z.B.V 800 Brandenburg.

BRITISH FORCES

Home forces.

General Alan Brooke

Chief of staff Lieutenant General Bernard Paget.

38th (Welsh) Infantry Division

21st Army Tank brigade.

IV corps Lieutenant General Francis Nosworthy.

2nd Armoured Division.

42nd (East Lancashire) infantry Division

31st independent infantry brigade group

VII corps Lieutenant General Andrew McNaughton of Canada.

1st Armoured Division

1st Canadian infantry Division

1st Army Tank Brigade.

Norther Command Lieutenant General Ronald Forbes Adams

1 corps Lieutenant General Harold Alexander.

1st infantry Division

2nd infantry Division

45th infantry Division

X corps Lieutenant General William Holmes.

54th (East Anglian) infantry Division

59th (Staffordshire) infantry Division

London District Lieutenant General Bertram Sergison-Brooke

20th independent infantry brigade (Guards)

24th Guards Brigade Group

3rd London Brigade.

Eastern Command.

Lieutenant General Laurence Carr.

II group Lieutenant General Edmund Osborne

18th infantry Division

52nd (Lowland) infantry Division

37th independent infantry Brigade

XI Corps Lieutenant General Hugh Massey.

15th (Scottish) infantry Division

55th (West Lancashire) infantry Division

XII Corps Lieutenant General Andrew Thorne.

1st London Division

43rd (Wessex) infantry Division

New Zealand Division

1st Motor Machinegun Brigade

29th independent infantry Division

Southern command lieutenant General Claude Auchinleck.

V corps Lieutenant General Bernard Montgomery

3rd infantry Division

4th infantry Division

50th (Northumbrian) infantry Division

VIII Corps Lieutenant General Harold Franklyn.

48th (South Midlands) division

70th independent infantry Brigade

Western Command General Robert Gordon Finlayson

2nd London Division

III Corps Lieutenant General James Marshall-Cornwall

5th infantry Division

3rd Motor machinegun Brigade

36th independent infantry Division

Scottish Command Lieutenant General Harold Carrington

46th infantry Division

51st (Highland) infantry Division

The whole plan relied on Germany having complete control of the English Channel, which in turn meant that Germany had to have control of the skies so that the Royal Air Force could not attack German ships crossing the channel, hence victory in the Battle of Britain was an integral part of the plan.

In August Goring Launched the Luftwaffe campaign to destroy the RAF and win control of the English Channel and the air over Southern England. In 1939 Reinicke spent five days on the study of the operation and set forth the following prerequisites.

Elimination or sealing off of the Royal Navy forces from landing and approach areas. Elimination of the Royal Air Force (RAF), destruction of all Royal Navy units in the coastal zone. Prevention of British Submarine action against the landing fleet.

On 16 July 1940 following Germany's swift and successful occupation of France and the low countries and growing impatient with Britain's outright rejection of his recent peace overtures. Hitler issued Fuhrer directive no: 16. Setting in motion preparations for a landing in Britain, he prefaced the order by stating "as Britain, in spite of her hopeless military situation, still shows no sign of willingness to come to terms, I have decided to prepare, and if necessary to carry out, a landing operation against her. The aim of this operation is to eliminate the English motherland as a base from which the war against Germany can be continued and if necessary, to occupy the country completely. Hitler's directive set four conditions for the invasion to occur.

The RAF was to be "beaten down in its morale and in fact, that it can no longer display any appreciable aggressive force in opposition to the German crossing". The English Channel was to be swept of British Mines and the Strait of Dover must be blocked at both ends by German Mines.

The coastal zone between occupied France and England must be dominated by heavy artillery. The Royal Navy must be sufficiently engaged in the North Sea and the Mediterranean so that it could not intervene in the crossing, British home squadrons must be damaged or destroyed by air and torpedo attacks.

Operation Sea Lion looked simple in theory, Britain should have been an easy target. The Luftwaffe was very experienced in modern warfare. All three branches of the German military had guessed that an invasion would be needed before Hitler gave the order, they had started on their own plans. The German Navy was able to provide its invasion fleet with the maximum protection. Once reinforcements had landed the advance northward was to begin but London would have been bypassed until resistance in the rest of Britain collapsed. However, for all the work done by the military on a projected invasion of Britain, it seems that Hitler had little enthusiasm for it.

On 17 June 1940, the navy received a communique that informed them that: "With regards to the landing in Britain the Fuhrer has not up to now expressed an intention, as he fully appreciates the unusual difficulties of such an operation. Therefore, even this time, no preparatory work of any kind has been carried out in the Wehrmacht high command".

On 21 June 1940, the navy was told that the Army General Staff, "is not concerning itself with the question of England. Considers execution impossible. Does not know how the operation is to be conducted from the Southern area."

Hitler spoke with great admiration of the British empire, of the necessity for its existence, and all the civilisation that Britain had brought in to the world." it was only when it became clear that Britain would not sign peace terms that Hitler gave his backing to an invasion. On 2 July 1940 Hitler gave his first tentative orders regarding a possible invasion of Britain. It stated that.

"A landing in England is possible, providing that air superiority can be attained and certain other necessary conditions fulfilled..... All the preparations must be made on the basis that the invasion is still only a plan, and has not yet been decided upon" HITLER JULY 2 1940.

On July 13 the army chiefs presented their plans, they were so confident of success that they believed that Britain would be occupied within a month. At a meeting with his service chiefs on July 21st Hitler made it clear that he recognised that the plan had its dangers, especially by Reader but he was keen to press on with the plan so he could turn his full attention to Russia once Britain had been defeated.

Hitler wanted Sea Lion to be over by mid-September, his naval chiefs believed that any invasion could not start until mid-September, several postponements took place through into September on the grounds that the essential conditions did not exist. The Luftwaffe's failure to achieve air superiority in the Battle of Britain forced Hitler to postpone the operation. A number of German General Staff members believed that Sea Lion was not going to succeed. Admiral Karl Donitz believed air superiority was 'not enough'. He stated "We possessed neither control of the air or the sea, nor were we in any position to gain it." Reader supplied a list of reasons why the invasion could not go ahead before mid-September 1940. (Clearance of shipping lanes of mines, getting invasion barges ready ETC) and won the support of the army.

Hitler ordered that as long as Germany controlled the sky, operation sea lion would go ahead starting on September 15th 1940, therefore the invasion depended entirely on whether Goring's Luftwaffe could defeat the RAF, The failure of the Germans to defeat the RAF had led to the cancellation of the operation, which was announced on 17 September 1940, but it was never formally cancelled, instead it was postponed indefinitely.

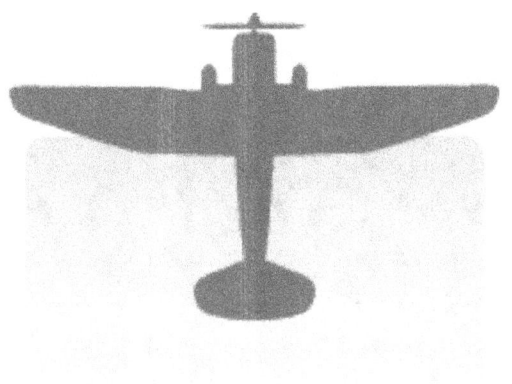

7

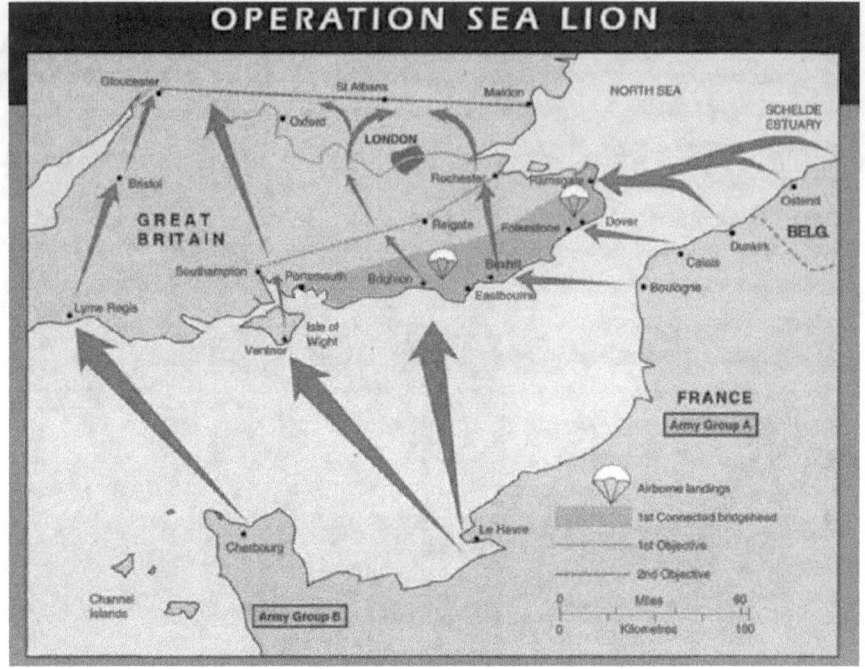

One of the interesting issues to come out of this episode was the inability of the three units that made up the German military to either work together or support one another. Primarily the chiefs of the army railed against Reader while he and his chiefs criticised the plans of the army, the Luftwaffe took the view, though it was primarily Goring's, that any success depended on the Luftwaffe conquering the skies. Even the Royal Navy had been neutralised, the chances of a successful amphibious invasion across the channel were remote. The Germans had no specialised landing craft, and had to rely primarily on River Barges to lift troops and supplies for the landing. This would have limited the quantity of artillery and tanks that could be transported, and restricted operations to times of good weather. The barges were not designed for use in open sea and, even in almost perfect conditions, they would be very slow and vulnerable to attack. Another key point that came out this episode in the war, was that Hitler's seeming refusal to listen to his military commanders, and wanting things done his way. This came out of the success the military had against Poland and the notions of Western Europe, countries attacked without the overwhelming support of the military, but attacked because Hitler instinctively knew they would win, or so he believed.

No one knew whether seal-ion would have succeeded or not, had it been launched, the sea and wind conditions on and over the channel from 19 to 26 September, where the invasion was to take place was good over-all. From the night of 27 September strong northerly winds prevailed, making passage more hazardous, calm conditions returned on 11-12 October and again 16-20 October. After that, light easterly winds prevailed, which actually would have assisted any invasion craft travelling from the continent towards the invasion beaches.

But by the end of October very strong South-Westerly winds (Force8) would prohibit any non-seagoing craft from risking a channel crossing. At least 20-25 German spies were sent to England by boat or parachute to gather information on the British coastal defences under the codename operation Lena many of the agents spoke limited English. All agents were quickly captured and may were convinced to defect by MI5' s Double-Cross system, providing disinformation to their German superiors.

Famous speeches of the Battle of Britain.

British Prime Minister Winston Churchill on 20 August 1940 made a war time speech, "never in the field of human conflict has so much been owed by so many to so few" referring to the ongoing efforts of the Royal Air Forces crews who were at the time fighting the Luftwaffe above the towns and cities of Great Britain.

In The battle of Britain he also made this speech. Upon this battle depends the survival of Cristian civilisation,

Upon it depend our own British life and the long continuity of our institutions, and our empire, The whole fury and might of the enemy must very soon be turned on us, Hitler knows that he will have to break us in this island, or loose the war, If we can stand up to him, all Europe may be freed, and the life of the world may move forward into broad and sunlit uplands, but if we fall, then the whole world, including the United States, and all that we have known and cared for, will sink into the abyss of a new dark age made more sinister and perhaps more prolonged by the lights of perverted science, let us therefore brace ourselves to our duty, and so bare ourselves that if the British empire and commonwealth lasts for a thousand years, men will still say

"This was their finest hour"

4 June 1940 in the House of Commons, after the Dunkirk evacuation, Churchill calm the nation's euphoria and stiffens its resolve.

"Even though large tracts of Europe and many old and famous states have fallen or may fall into the grip of the Gestapo and all the odious apparatus of Nazi rule, we shall not flag or fail. We shall go on to the end, we shall fight them in France, we shall fight them on the seas and oceans, we shall fight them with growing confidence and growing strength in the air, we shall defend our island, whatever the cost may be, we shall fight them on the beaches, we shall fight them on the landing grounds, we shall fight in the fields and in the streets, we shall fight in the hills, we shall never surrender.

20 August 1940 in the House of Commons, as the Battle of Britain Climaxes, Churchill praises the bravery of the RAF.

The gratitude of every home in our island, in our empire, and indeed throughout the world, except in the abodes of the guilty, goes out to the British airmen who, undaunted by odds, unwearied in their in their constant challenge and mortal danger, are turning the tide of the world war by their prowess and by their devotion. Never in the field of human conflict was so much owed by so many to so few.

Adolf Hitler

A portion of Hitler's speech at the sportsplast September

4 1940.

It is a wonderful thing to see our nation at war, in it's fairly disciple state. This is exactly what we are now experiencing at this time, as Mr Churchill is demonstrating to us the aerial night attacks which he has consorted.

He is not doing this because these air raids might be particularly effective, but because his air force cannot fly over German territory in daylight. Whereas German aviators and German planes fly over English soil daily, there is hardly a single Englishman who comes across the North Sea in daytime.

They therefore come during the night and as you know, release there bombs indiscriminately and without any plan on residential areas, farm houses and villages. Where ever they see a sign of light, a bomb is dropped on it. For three months past, I have not ordered any answer to be given, thinking that they would stop this nonsensical behaviour, Mr Churchill has taken this to be a sign of our weakness. You will understand that we shall now give a reply, night for night, and with increasing force.

And if the British Air Force drops two, three or four thousand kilos of bombs then we shall now drop 150,000. 180,000, 230,000. 300,000 or 400,000 kilo's or more, in one night, if they declare that they will attack our cities on a large scale, we will erase theirs: we will put a stop to the game of these night pirates, as god is our witness. The hour will come when one or the other of us will crumble, and that one will not be the National Socialist Germany. I have already carried through such a struggle once in my life, up to the final consequences, and this then led to the collapse of the enemy who is now sitting there in England on Europe's last island.

Adolf Hitler addressing a rally after the bombing of berlin stated:

> If they send over a hundred bombers to bomb our cities..... Then we shall send a thousand plane to bomb theirs. And if they think that they can destroy our cities....
>
> Then we shall wipe theirs from the face of the earth.

Adolf Hitler on deciding that London should be Bombed. September 1940.

Will not the British learn, their bombers come and kill innocent German People, and I have given them fair warning. We have told you before, that the nights when the British bombers do not attack our capital, our glorious Luftwaffe has forcibly stopped the British bombers in their tracks and they had to turn for home. But now the time is right, the British Air force is down to its last reserves, they cry for pity, and I will give them pity for I will wipe London from the face of the earth. I want fire everywhere, thousands of them and then they will unite in one gigantic area of conflagration.

RECAP OF BATTLE OF BRITAIN

Battle of Britain came to head because Hitler's peace overture was rejected by Winston Churchill, so he had stated that Britain was a weak nation with very few defences, making Britain an easily overcome nation, he was not expecting the skill and determination of our airmen, and naval personnel and army personnel.

Britain was better equipped with more planes than he was told by his own spies, ultimately losing the Battle of Britain. Marking the first defeat of Hitler's military forces. The Battle of Britain is justifiably remembered as Britain's "FINEST HOUR".

Although a huge number of men and women were involved in the Battle, whether working in factories, manning the radar stations, repairing aircraft or working in the control rooms. The crucial part of the fighting was carried out by around 1,000 fighter pilots on each side at any one time, when the battle began everybody expected the Germans would soon attempt to invade Britain.

The Germans did launch some spectacular attacks against important British industries, but could not destroy the British industrial potential, and made little systematic effort to do so. For the participants it seemed as if there was a narrow margin between victory and defeat. By the end of the Battle of Britain it was clear that the Germans would not be invaded in 1940, and that probably missed their best chance to do so.

31st October was the official end of the Battle of Britain but bombing continued on London. If Britain had been defeated then Hitler wouldn't have needed to prop up the Italians in the Mediterranean and North Africa, the United States would probably not have entered the war against Hitler, and even if it had done wouldn't have had the UK to use as a base. Dowding's 'chicks', the famous few, won one of the most significant military victories in history.

The British victory in the Battle of Britain was achieved at a heavy cost.

CREDITATION'S

All information and photographs in this book is are from the following websites and the author would like to thank them for their information.

www.wikipedia.org, www.historylearningsite.co.uk, www.history.com, www.militaryhistory.com, www.ww2db.com www.nzetc.victoria.ac.nk, www.bbc.co.uk/history www.battleofbritain1940.net, www. 1900. org.uk, www.historyplace.com, wwwrafmuseum.org.uk, www.winstonchurchill.org, www.historyextra.com.

Some references were from a book written by Nigel Cawthorne named Battles of WWII.

This book was compiled with the respect to all those who fought in and lived through and all those who died during the Battle of Britain, may they rest in peace and with massive respect to THE FEW, who fought day and night in the air above to keep our country and this great nation safe from the Nazi Luftwaffe. And all the leaders during this Battle and all our great Armed Forces.

Prototype spitfire

With thanks to all websites used for thier information on compiling my books.

www.battleofbritain1940. net
www.wikipedia.com

BIBLIOGRAPHY

Anderson Shelter:
https:// www.andersonshelters.org.uk/

air raid shelter in Stalham street 1940
http:// www.portcities.org.uk/ london/ server/ show/ conMediaFile. 909/ Airraid-shelter-in-Stalham-Street-1940. html

Winston Churchill
https:// en.wikipedia.org/ wiki/ Winston_Churchill#/ media/ File:Sir_ Winston_Churchill_-_19086236948. jpg

Hugh Dowding
https:// en.wikipedia.org/ wiki/ Hugh_Dowding#/ media/ File:Hugh_ Dowding.jpg
Air Marshal Keith Park
https:// en.wikipedia.org/ wiki/ Keith_Park#/media/File:Air_ Marshal_Sir_Keith_Park.jpg

Air Chief Marshal Trafford Leigh-Mallory
https:// www.npg.org.uk/ collections/ search/ portrait/ mw101997/ Sir- Trafford-Leigh-Leigh-Mallory

Vice Air Marshal Sir Christopher Quintin Brand
https:// www.npg.org.uk/ collections/ search/ portrait/ mw110870/ Sir- Christopher-Joseph-Quintin-Brand? LinkID = mp78187& role = sit& rNo = 0

Vice Air Marshal Richard Ernest Saul
https:// en.wikipedia.org/ wiki/ Richard_Saul#/ media/ File:Air_ Vice-Marshal_Richard_Saul.jpg

William Lyon Mackenzie King
https:// en.wikipedia.org/ wiki/ William_Lyon_Mackenzie_ King#/ media/ File:WilliamLyonMackenzieKing.jpg

Air Chief Marshal Lloyd Samuel Breadner
https:// i0. wp.com/ www.junobeach.org/ wp-content/ uploads/ 2014/ 03/ people_canada_breadner.jpg

Adolf Hitler
https:// en.wikipedia.org/ wiki/ Adolf_Hitler#/ media/ File:Hitler_ portrait_crop.jpg

Wilhelm Bodewin Johann Gustav Keitel
https:// en.wikipedia.org/ wiki/ Wilhelm_Keitel#/ media/ File: Bundesarchiv_Bild_183-H30220,_Wilhelm_Keitel.jpg

Herman Goring
https:// en.wikipedia.org/ wiki/ Hermann_G% C3% B6ring#/ media/ File:Hermann_G% C3% B6ring_-_R% C3% B6hr.jpg

Albert Kesselring
https:// en.wikipedia.org/ wiki/ Albert_Kesselring#/ media/ File: Bundesarchiv_Bild_183-R93434,_Albert_Kesselring.jpg

Hugo Sperrle
https:// www.britannica.com/ biography/ Hugo-Sperrle

Benito Mussolini
https:// www.thinglink.com/ scene/ 1010968477407641602

Bomb Damage
https:// ww2db.com/ battle_spec.php? battle_id = 95

Bomb Damage 1
https:// www.spectator.co.uk/ 2013/ 10/ the-bombing-war-by-richard- overy-review/

www.ingramcontent.com/pod-product-compliance
Lightning Source LLC
Chambersburg PA
CBHW071457070526
44578CB00001B/373